HOTEL VALHALLA
GUIDE TO THE NORSE WORLDS

HOTEL VALHALLA

GUIDE TO THE NORSE WORLDS

AN OFFICIAL MAGNUS CHASE COMPANION BOOK

RICK RIORDAN

PUFFIN

A special thank you to Stephanie True Peters
for her help with this book

PUFFIN BOOKS

UK | USA | Canada | Ireland | Australia
India | New Zealand | South Africa

Puffin Books is part of the Penguin Random House group of companies
whose addresses can be found at global.penguinrandomhouse.com.

www.penguin.co.uk   www.puffin.co.uk   www.ladybird.co.uk

First published in the USA by Disney • Hyperion, an imprint
of Disney Book Group, and in Great Britain by Puffin Books 2016

001

Text copyright © Rick Riordan, 2016
Illustrations copyright © Yori Elita Narpati, 2016

The moral right of the author and illustrator has been asserted

Printed in Great Britain by Clays Ltd, St Ives plc

A CIP catalogue record for this book is available from the British Library

HARDBACK ISBN:
978–0–141–37653–0

INTERNATIONAL PAPERBACK ISBN:
978–0–141–37727–8

All correspondence to
Puffin Books, Penguin Random House Children's
80 Strand, London WC2R 0RL

For all einherjar
May you prove worthy of Valhalla

CONTENTS

A WORD FROM THE MANAGER 2

WHAT IN THE WORLDS? 5

THE GODS AND GODDESSES 11

   ODIN 14

   THOR 22

   LOKI 28

   FREY 34

   FREYA 39

   SKIRNIR 46

   MIMIR 50

   HEL 55

   HEIMDALL 58

   RAN 60

   FRIGG PLUS BALDER, HOD, IDUN

   AND HONIR 63

   TYR 74

   ULLER 76

   NJORD 78

MYTHICAL BEINGS 79

    GIANTS 82

      SURT 82

      YMIR 85

      UTGARD-LOKI 88

      GERD 93

    ELVES 96

    DWARVES 100

    VALKYRIES 104

    THE NORNS 110

FANTASTIC CREATURES 113

    NIDHOGG, EAGLE AND RATATOSK 114

    HEIDRUN, EIKTHRYMIR AND SAEHRIMNIR ... 118

    SLEIPNIR 125

    JORMUNGAND 128

    FENRIS WOLF 132

    OTIS AND MARVIN 138

A FINAL WORD FROM THE MANAGER 142

PRONUNCIATION GUIDE 145

GLOSSARY 149

HOTEL VALHALLA

VALHALLA

GUIDE TO THE NORSE WORLDS

HOTEL VALHALLA

A Word from the Manager

Dear Valued Guest,

On behalf of the staff, welcome to Hotel Valhalla. We recognize that there were other options for your afterlife. We thank you for the selfless sacrifice that landed you here among Odin's chosen warriors instead of elsewhere.

You will encounter many powerful deities, magical beings and fantastic creatures as an *einherji*. You may have questions about them. You may decide to ask me those questions. In fact, if more than a millennium of experience is any indication, you *will* ask me. Of course, as manager of this fine establishment, I'll be happy to answer them. But I'll be even happier if you consult this guide before you ring the front desk. I do have a hotel to run, after all.

With insightful interviews and scintillating stories, insider information and random remarks, this book allows you to explore the lives of our worlds' inhabitants from the comfort of your room. As you read, you may wish to ponder the possibility of your own heroic tale finding a page in future editions of this book.* Will your deeds earn you a coveted seat at the thanes' table, or will they be less than satisfactory, securing your role as servant to those who answer Odin's call? If the former, I will be the first to welcome you, for I myself am a thane. If the latter, please confer with Hunding the bellhop about your duties.

For now, though, sit back, relax and enjoy your ongoing death, your daily resurrection and your everlasting stay here.

Helgi
MANAGER OF HOTEL VALHALLA
SINCE 749 C.E.

---

* All publications and the proceeds thereof will become the property of Hotel Valhalla.

WHAT IN THE WORLDS?
by Hunding
HOTEL VALHALLA BELLHOP SINCE 749 C.E.

To be honest, I'm not great with words, so I wasn't keen on writing anything for this book. But Helgi told me to, and I have to do what Helgi tells me, because – well, that's a story for another time. Maybe someday I'll write it down. But probably not.

I'm supposed to tell you where we live. We live in a tree. It's a really, really big tree called *Yggdrasil*. It has a name because it's important, and all important things have names. I don't know who named it. Come to think of it, I don't know who named anything. Is there a god for that?

Yggdrasil is also known as the World Tree. Not only is that easier to pronounce, it's a spot-on description, because the branches hold nine – count 'em, *nine* – worlds: *Asgard, Vanaheim, Midgard, Alfheim, Jotunheim, Nidavellir, Muspellheim, Niflheim* and *Helheim*. When I first joined the hotel staff, I had trouble remembering their names. So I came up with this handy mnemonic device: A Very Mean Ant Just Nibbled My Nose Hair. *A* stands for Asgard, *V* for Vanaheim and so on. Get it? You can use my special sentence if you want. Just leave me chocolate in return.

Now, a little bit about each world:

ASGARD: This is the realm of the *Aesir*, warrior gods and goddesses. These deities – *Odin*, *Thor* and *Frigg*, among others – reside in palaces made of silver, gold and other precious materials. Hotel *Valhalla*, the beloved afterlife residence of the *einherjar*, the soldiers in Odin's eternal army, is within this world.

VANAHEIM: Home of the *Vanir*, the nature gods and goddesses, this world is warm and sunny, filled with lush green meadowland. *Folkvanger*, the flower-child afterlife equivalent of Valhalla, is within this realm. The Vanir goddess *Freya* rules over Folkvanger from her palace *Sessrumnir*, or Hall of Many Seats, which is an upside-down ship crafted of gold and silver.

MIDGARD: If you are human, this is where you once lived. Midgard rests in Yggdrasil's branches and is connected to Asgard via the *Bifrost*, a massive bridge constructed from a single rainbow. The city of Boston, Massachusetts, is very close to Yggdrasil's trunk, making it a useful point of entry to and exit from the other worlds.

ALFHEIM: The home of the light elves, Alfheim resembles Midgard in many ways except that elves, not humans, live here, and there is no night. The Vanir god *Frey* rules over it. Alfheim is kind of an upscale neighbourhood, so be on your best behaviour if you visit. Otherwise you might get arrested for loitering, or trespassing, or just . . . you know, not being an elf.

JOTUNHEIM: The world of the giants, or *jotun*, is primarily mountainous, with great drifts of snow, half-frozen rivers and lakes, and, well, giants. Giants are large and not particularly careful about where they step. Be cautious travelling in Jotunheim. I've had more than one friend flattened under a giant's boot.

NIDAVELLIR: The underground realm of the dwarves, this world is chilly and dark because the only natural light comes from a special glowing moss. The buildings are equally gloomy, though the furnishings within are one-of-a-kind creations, for dwarves are master craftsmen. If you want to pick up a souvenir, like a magic hammer or a foldable boat, be prepared to pay handsomely. Dwarves take gold, all major credit cards and your head (if you lose a wager with them). One section of Nidavellir is called *Svartalfheim*, the land of the 'dark elves', but this isn't really a separate world, and the svartalfs aren't actually elves. They are dwarves who have some Vanir blood since they descended from Freya. (Long story. Freya doesn't like to talk about it.)

MUSPELLHEIM: This is the land where fire giants and demons dwell. Imagine the surface of the sun, populated with angry, heavily armed burning people. *Surt*, the lord of the fire giants, rules this world and doesn't appreciate visitors. Best to steer clear.

NIFLHEIM: An inhospitable, frigid region of mist, ice and fog, it is where the frost giants often reside. Great place to make an ice sculpture or store meat if you run out of room in your freezer. However, since high summer temperatures hover at around −30 degrees Fahrenheit, I'd wear your warmies.

HELHEIM: The dead who don't go to Valhalla or Folkvanger end up here. It's a cold, dark, lifeless place, full of miserable souls who died of old age or sickness. To get there, you have to ride down an icy road into the pitch-black Valley of Death, cross the River Gjoll on an iron bridge guarded by a giantess, somehow get across the Wall of Corpses and finally arrive at the Hall of *Hel*, the goddess of the dishonourable dead, where you'll be served famine, hunger and misery for breakfast, lunch and dinner. Suffice to say, Helheim rarely makes it on the list of top vacation spots for the Nine Worlds.

A few other points of interest: at the roots of Yggdrasil is a magical well of knowledge, overseen by the ancient god *Mimir* (or at least Mimir's head, because that's all that's left of him). Drink from the well, and you can learn important stuff. You have to pay Mimir for the drink, though, and the price isn't cheap. Just ask Odin. (But I'd wait until he's in a good mood before asking.)

Travel among the worlds is allowed, though some restrictions may apply. There's one place you shouldn't visit, however, and that's the massive abyss of nothingness called *Ginnungagap*. True story: long ago, before anything was anything, frost from Niflheim spread into Ginnungagap and met with fire coming from Muspellheim. No big surprise, the frost melted. Some drops turned into a humungous giant named *Ymir*. A few generations later, Odin and his brothers *Vili* and *Ve* killed Ymir and turned his body parts into Midgard's oceans, sky, earth and plants. Ever since then, the giants have hated the gods. Moral of the story: avoid Ginnungagap. You just never know what might happen there.

THE
GODS AND GODDESSES

by Hunding

M e again. Did you think my contribution began and ended with the explanation of the Nine Worlds? Apparently, we were both wrong.

So, the gods and goddesses. These divine beings permeate all aspects of our cosmos. They belong to one of two tribes, the Aesir or the Vanir. The Aesir are warriors. They dwell in Asgard and handle most aspects of law and order – defending it in battle, maintaining it through their swift and often deadly system of justice and, on occasion, disrupting it by means of pranks, tricks and crimes. They cherish loyalty, honour and a 'fight for what's right' sensibility above all else. (Except when they are engaged in pranks, tricks and crimes.) A good time to be around the Aesir is on the battlefield. They will always have your back. A bad time to be around the Aesir is when they're drinking mead together. Then the insults start flying, and wow – some of those Aesir insults can make your ears bleed.

The more peaceful Vanir oversee the nature side of things, such as fertility, the seasons, crop growth and the like, from their home world of Vanaheim. They appreciate groovy, laid-back calm and finely crafted macramé handbags.

The Vanir are not complete pacifists, however. Take the Aesir–Vanir war. According to historic accounts, it was triggered by a sorceress from Vanaheim, who some say was Freya herself. The witch travelled the worlds performing elf magic, or *alf seidr*. She put on a show in Asgard for Odin and the other gods. The Aesir were impressed with her powers until they realized she was using them for one purpose: to obtain their gold. (No offence, Freya, but your lust for gold is probably how the rumours about you being the sorceress got started.)

Her greed offended the Aesir. So they did the only logical thing: they burned her. Three times, actually. Each time, she popped out of the flames uncharred. Finally, though, she'd had enough. She returned to Vanaheim, posted a one-star rating for her stay in Asgard and *boom* – war erupted.

No one knows how long the two tribes fought. But eventually both sides got sick and tired of it. They called a truce. To seal the deal, they did a deity hostage exchange – Freya, Frey and their dad, *Njord* of Vanaheim, for Asgard's Mimir and *Honir*. I'd like to say that it all worked out fine, but I suspect Mimir would disagree since he got his head cut off for being sassy with the Vanir. And how Freya wound up back in Vanaheim in charge of Folkvanger is anyone's guess.

But that's the divine for you; they operate by their own set of rules. Speaking of which, read on to learn more about the Norse deities.

ODIN

TYPE: God

HOME WORLD: Asgard

APPEARANCE: A weathered warrior. Muscular and barrel-chested. Close-cropped grey hair and tidy, square-cut beard. Eyepatch over left eye; right eye is deep blue. Exudes power and wisdom.

FAMILY: Married to the goddess Frigg and father of many sons, including the god *Balder*

BEST KNOWN FOR: Being the All-Father, king of the gods, the god of war and death and of poetry and wisdom. Oversees Valhalla, where he receives half of those who die bravely in battle, the einherjar. Can shape-shift. Continually seeking new knowledge, he often consults the disembodied head of the wise being Mimir for advice. Author of many books, including his latest, *Seven Heroic Qualities.*

FAVOURITE WEAPON: Odin is frequently seen with his spear, *Gungnir.* (Told you everything important here has a name.)

ANIMAL COMPANIONS: Odin is often accompanied by the wolves *Geri* and *Freki* and the ravens *Huginn* and *Muninn,* who bring him information from all over Midgard. He rides the flying eight-legged steed *Sleipnir* across the sky and into the underworld.

MY SIT-DOWN WITH ODIN
by Snorri Sturluson
RESIDENT OF HOTEL VALHALLA SINCE 1241 C.E.

As an author, historian and sometime poet in life, and a *thane* in good standing in death, I've had the privilege of conversing with our deities many times over the last centuries. These chats became the basis of my book, *The Prose Edda* (available for purchase online and in better bookstores), which contains highly readable explanations of our most famous 'myths' and insights about our celebrated heroes. When Helgi told me he was putting a guide to our worlds in every room of the hotel, I assumed he meant my *Edda*. But apparently he was looking for something with a more modern flair. He asked if I could recommend someone to interview our top-level gods and goddesses. No doubt he thought the task was beneath me, but I welcomed the opportunity for some one-on-one time with the deities. Naturally, my first conversation was with Odin, the All-Father himself. We met not at the High Seat *Hlidskjalf* as I'd suggested but in an out-of-the-way, unassuming Midgard café.

[Editor's Note: *Snorri Sturluson* has had issues with accuracy in the past. To ensure this is not an issue with this and other interviews recorded in this book, a raven scribe accompanied him to his meetings. The transcripts therefore include impartial observations as well as the conversations themselves.]

SNORRI STURLUSON: Thank you, my lord, for agreeing to talk to me. I'm certain readers will be extremely interested in whatever you say.

ODIN: Probably.

SS: May I ask my first question?

O: You just did.

SS [laughing delightedly]: Oh, you got me that time! Wise and witty, all in one package! But now to the question. Odin, tell us, in your own words . . . what was it like when you lost your eye?

O [cheerfully]: I didn't lose it, Snorri. I gouged it out with my own fingers.

SS [looking green]: In . . . deed. And, erm, what was that like?

O: Not fun. But I got something worthwhile in exchange for it.

SS: And that was?

O: This cool eyepatch.

SS: Ah. Nothing else?

O: Oh, I got a sip of water from the well of knowledge at Yggdrasil's roots, too. Mimir, the severed head, gave it to me himself.

SS [grandly]: And that was the first heroic step on your everlasting quest for wisdom!

O: Sure. [Scratches his beard thoughtfully.] Makes you wonder, though, doesn't it?

SS [leaning forward]: Wonder what, Lord Odin?

O: What Mimir did with my eye. [Shrugs.]

SS: A mystery that may never be solved. Speaking of mysteries, you once hanged yourself to gain wisdom. We're all dying to know –

O: *'Dying to know'!* Good one, Snorri!

SS: What? Oh. Yes, I see. So, can you tell us the story behind you hanging yourself for nine days to unlock the secret of runes?

O: Of course. [Pause.] I hanged myself for nine days to unlock the secret of runes.

SS: Yes, but why did you *hang* yourself?

O: To unlock the secret of runes.

SS: Er, yes. Fascinating.

O: But all that is ancient history, Snorri, as is the tale about how I stole and drank a vat of mead made from god spittle to become a poet.

SS [looking green]: God spittle.

O: Well, *technically*, the mead was made with honey and . . . well, let's call it a secret ingredient.* [Winks.]

SS: Sounds delicious.

O: It was nauseating. I spat some out while soaring above Midgard. Drops of it are still down there. A few humans accidentally swallow it now and again. Those who do

---

* Unconfirmed rumours claim the secret ingredient was the blood of *Kvasir*, a wise god who arose fully formed from a vat of divine spittle. The saliva itself came from the gods and goddesses, who took turns loogying into the vat to seal the truce that ended the Aesir–Vanir war. Two nasty dwarves, *Fjalar* and *Gjalar,* killed Kvasir and mixed his blood with honey to make the mead. The term 'bloodthirsty' may originate with this event.

become world-renowned poets and scholars. [Cups hands and shouts towards Midgard.] Shakespeare, Longfellow, Silverstein – you're welcome!

SS: World-renowned poets and scholars, eh? [Chuckles in a self-deprecating manner.] You must think I had a taste of it myself!

O: That possibility has never once crossed my mind.

SS: Ah. Well. Ancient history, as you say. Perhaps you'd like to tell us about your latest quests for wisdom and knowledge instead?

O: I'd like to tell you many things, Snorri. But to answer your question: I've started a spoken-word poetry group with some of my einherjar. Performances every Thor's Day night in the Feast Hall of the Slain, with light *Saehrimnir* refreshments to follow. The *Norns* are scheduled to make a guest appearance soon, which should prove interesting. Also, I'm taking Zumba classes to understand why in My Name they're so popular. Finally, I'm researching the magical symbol known in Midgard as [taps first two fingers of right hand against the first two fingers of left hand] *hashtag*. From what I've gleaned, when combined with other words, *hashtag* has the power to distract the mind from more important matters. If I'm right, I'll make hashtag the subject of my next book. The working title is . . . wait for it . . . *Hashtag*.

SS: An inspired choice, Lord Odin.

O: Yes, I know.

Sadly, our interview came to an abrupt conclusion at this point. Odin was called away on a matter of great Aesir importance. He couldn't reveal the nature of the emergency, but I'm quite certain I heard the words *hammer* and *missing*.

THOR

TYPE: God

HOME WORLD: Asgard

APPEARANCE: Bulging tattooed biceps, mountainous shoulders, massive chest and carrot-coloured hair. Wears a rarely washed sleeveless leather jerkin and leather trousers, a chain-mail vest, a magic belt and iron gauntlets. His finger knuckles are also tattooed.

FAMILY: Thor sired many children; his favourite sons are *Magni* and *Modi*. He had other offspring with his wife, the goddess *Sif*.

BEST KNOWN FOR: Being the god of thunder. He has a weekday named after him. His creative cusswords and explosive farts are almost as legendary as his strength, with which he protects humankind. Binge-watches Midgard television procedurals in his spare time.

FAVOURITE WEAPON: His mountain-crushing hammer, *Mjolnir*, which also has the ability to pick up Wi-Fi and broadcast television in high resolution. If he were ever to lose it, he'd miss out on his favourite shows. Oh, and also, the Nine Worlds would be in serious trouble. He has a staff made of giant-forged iron as a backup.

ANIMAL COMPANIONS: *Tanngnjóstr* (meaning 'Teeth Grinder'; you can call him *Otis*) and *Tanngrisnr* (meaning 'Snarler'; just use *Marvin*), two talking goats that can be killed, cooked, eaten and then resurrected. Convenient when you are hungry while on the road.

A HERO AND A HAMMER
by John Henry

RESIDENT OF HOTEL VALHALLA SINCE 1871 C.E.

Growing up, I never suspected I was the son of the Norse god of thunder. Why would I? I was born in America – West Virginia, North Carolina, I'm not exactly sure where – 'round about 1840 or so. Oh, did I mention? My mamma was a slave. That means I was a slave, too.

And my daddy? In my heart, he was the man my mamma was married to, the man who raised me and loved me like his own. But, as it turns out, we weren't blood kin.

When I was born, Thor sent me an anonymous gift – Mjolnir Junior, a tiny version of his own hammer, though I didn't know what it was then. There was enough of him in me that I took to that hammer like a duck to water, which is to say I pounded the living daylights out of anything and everything. (I ate, farted and snored like Thor, too. Still do. No cussing, though. My mamma raised me right.)

As I grew, so did that hammer. I reckon that should have been a clue that it was magic. But greater things were on my mind in those days. The Civil War, for one, and later the end of slavery. I was in my twenties when I became a freeman. With my mamma's blessing in my ears and her kiss on my forehead, I stuck my hammer in my belt and set off to make my way in the world.

I'd been travelling for a while when I met up with a man. Biggest fella I'd ever seen. Tall and wide, with tattooed arms the size of tree trunks and shoulders like granite. Matted red hair and a thick beard to match. One whiff of him, though, and I was ready to hightail it in the other direction. But something stopped me. He had a hammer in his hand. A hammer just like mine.

So I sat with him by his fire. We shared a meal of goat stew and a mug of a drink he called mead. (He called the stew Otis. I found out why when I got to Valhalla.) We traded stories. He told a whopper about some thief named *Thrym* who once stole his hammer. He played a trick on Thrym to get it back. Pretended to be the woman Thrym wanted to marry – bridal gown and all! Just before the ceremony, Thrym gave his 'bride' the stolen hammer as a token of his love. Thor grabbed it and bashed Thrym in the head. Took out the groomsmen, the guests and the cake, too.

You might think hearing that story would put me on guard. But, for some reason, I trusted the big fella. And he trusted me. When I asked if I could try his hammer, he let out a snort of laughter punctuated with a colossal fart. 'Be my guest!'

I passed out from the strain of trying to lift it. When I came to, he and his hammer were gone. But he left a note behind. Trouble is, back then, I couldn't read. So I just tucked the paper in my pocket.

Not long after, my hammering skill got me a job driving steel spikes for the railway. Mile after mile, month after month, I pounded track into place. I was the best worker of all – until the day a smooth-talking, scar-faced salesman rode into town. He was selling steam-powered drills he claimed were faster and stronger than any steel-driving man. I couldn't read, but I saw the writing on the wall. His machine was going to put me and plenty of others out of work.

I had no choice but to try to show him up. I bet him that, in one day's time, my hammer and I could lay more track, and through a mountain no less, than his machine. If he won, the railway would buy his machines. If I won, he would leave and never come back. He took my bet.

That night, my redheaded friend showed up at my tent. 'John Henry,' he said, 'I know this salesman. He's a [expletives deleted] trickster, and [expletives deleted] tricksters don't play fair. So I'm going to lend you something to even the odds.'

He took off his belt and looped it around my waist. The minute it touched my skin, power surged through my veins. He laid his hammer in my hands. This time, I wielded it with ease.

At dawn, I strode towards the tunnel. That scar-faced salesman raised an eyebrow when he saw the hammer. 'Well,' he said, 'this just got interesting.'

Here's what happened next: we competed. I won. And then I died. I landed here in Valhalla with the hammer in my hand – and the redheaded man's note in my pocket. A pretty lady on a strange smoky-looking horse read it to me:

This man is my son. Treat him right. If you don't, I'll bash your heads in.

It was signed *Thor*. And that's how I learned who my real daddy was.

LOKI

TYPE: God, born of two giants

HOME WORLD: Asgard

APPEARANCE: Messy hair in shades of red, yellow
and brown. Handsome except for a horribly scarred
face and lips marred by pierce holes.

FAMILY: The father of Hel; *Fenris Wolf*; the World
Serpent, *Jormungand*; *Narvi* and *Vali*, among others.
The mother of the eight-legged steed, Sleipnir.
(How's *that* for dysfunctional?)

BEST KNOWN FOR: Being a trickster, magician and shape-shifter. This smooth-talker is very dangerous. Currently, as punishment for engineering the death of the god Balder, he is lashed to boulders and tortured by venom dripping onto his face from a serpent's mouth. Still, he somehow manages to get around and cause trouble throughout the worlds.

DEALING WITH A
DEAL-BREAKER
by *Brokkr* the Dwarf

That *Loki*, he's some kind of handsome, huh? Until you see the scars on his face and the little pinholes above and below his lips. Betcha don't know how he got those holes. Cop a seat on that boulder, and I'll tell you about it.

So Loki, one day he's bored. He breaks into Thor's place to muck around with the thunder god's stuff. Not too smart, if you ask me. Anyway, Thor's not home, but his wife, Sif, is. Now Sif, she's this gorgeous platinum blonde. Well, not platinum so much as gold. Real pretty hair, though, and wicked long. Loki sneaks up behind her with a knife. She doesn't hear him, because she's asleep. He cuts off her hair, which was a rotten thing to do on account that she was so proud of it.

She wakes up, sees she's pretty much bald and starts crying her eyes out. Who walks in then, but Thor. Let me tell you, he's not the brightest coal in the kiln, if you get my drift. But even he can make out what's got Sif all upset. I mean, Loki is standing there with a knife in one hand and Sif's hair in the other. Calling Captain Obvious, am I right?

So Loki's caught red-handed. But he's a persuasive guy. He tells Thor, who is ready to pound him to a pulp with his fists, that he'll get Sif a wig that'll look even better than her real hair. Thor says okay, because what else is he going do, let his wife go around bald and crying? Hardly.

Only one place Loki can get a fine piece of craftsmanship like that, and that's right here in Nidavellir. So he hops on the tree at Asgard, changes branches in Alfheim and gets off at Nabbi's Tavern. He asks around and finds a couple of dwarves – Ivaldi's boys – to take the job. They make Sif a wig and, just to show off, throw in a magic spear and a ship that folds up so small it fits in a pocket.

You think Loki hoofs it back to Thor's palace with the goods? Nah. He's having a good time in Nidavellir. That's when me and my bro *Sindri* come into the story. Loki saunters into our shop and starts poking around. He shows us the wig, the spear and the ship and bets his head – no joke, his *head* – we can't make anything that good. Sindri and me take the bet, because we know our stuff is insanely awesome.

So we're firing up the kiln, hammering some

metal, kind of showing off for the god. He watches for a few minutes, then says he's going back to Asgard. What he really does? Turns into a horsefly and gets all up in our faces while we're working. We had, like, no clue it was him bugging us, but it didn't even matter. What we made *rocked*. First thing we pumped out was this boar with golden bristles that could run wicked fast. Second thing was a gold ring that makes eight copies of itself every ninth day. How fantastic is that? But the best thing we made was this hammer that always hits its target and boomerangs back to its owner.

So we bring the stuff to Asgard, looking for Loki, because he never showed to collect. We're confident, right, so we also bring a bag to put Loki's head in. Not that we think he's really going to pay up. Surprise, surprise, even though all the gods say the boar and the ring and the hammer are the coolest things ever and we totally win the bet, Loki tries to squirm out of the deal.

'I just promised you could take my *head* off,' Loki says. 'But I didn't say anything about my neck. Don't touch my neck!'

How are we supposed to cut a guy's head off without touching his neck?

'You're a cheat and a lying weasel,' Sindri says to him. 'So here's what we're going to do. We're going to make sure you can't talk anyone else into making stuff for you.'

Sindri and I jump him. Loki doesn't see it coming and falls like a ton of bricks. The other gods, they just look the other way while Sindri takes out his needle and thread and – well, you've seen Loki's mouth. Sure, he can talk *now*. Eventually he managed to tug the stitches out of his lips. But he wasn't saying a single thing when we left that day.

In case you're wondering, we gave the boar to Frey, the ring to Odin and the hammer to Thor. You don't hear much about the first two, but yeah . . . the hammer we made is *that* hammer.

FREY

TYPE: God

HOME WORLD: First Vanaheim, then Asgard after
the Aesir–Vanir War; now rules over Alfheim

APPEARANCE: Blue-eyed, blond and absurdly good-
looking in a tanned, unshaven, outdoorsy kind of
way. Leans towards flannel shirts, well-worn jeans
and hiking boots. Radiates warmth, peace and
contentment.

FAMILY: Son of Njord, the sea god; twin brother of
Freya; husband of the frost giantess *Gerd*

BEST KNOWN FOR: Being the god of spring and summer, and the lord of Alfheim. He's sunshine on a cloudy day. When it's cold outside, he's the month of May.

FAVOURITE WEAPON: *Sumarbrander*, the Sword of Summer (yay!). Unfortunately, he gave it away (boo!). A deer antler will do in a pinch.

ANIMAL COMPANION: When he isn't sailing his ship, which can be folded up to fit in a pocket and always has a favourable breeze, he can be seen riding a shining dwarf-made boar

THE RAP DUEL OF
JACK THE SWORD AND FREY

JACK

I'm Jack, the Sword of Summer,
  Sumarbrander, Blade of Frey.
That is, I *was* his, until he tossed
  me away.

                              FREY

                Jack, I did you wrong. You know
                    I'm feeling the guilt.

JACK

Yeah, right. Forget you, man. Talk
  to my hilt!

                              FREY

                Come on, Slice! Give me a chance.
                    At least let me explain
                    why I passed you off to *Skirnir* –

JACK

I know why. You were insane.
You sat on Odin's throne to search
  for Freya, your lost sister.
A giantess caught your eye. So
  much for Freya. You just dissed
  her.

FREY

       Gerd was gorgeous. Total hottie. I

              dream of her still.

          Shining face, lovely hair –

JACK

I think I'm going to be ill.

FREY

       I know you've suffered, Blade

       of Frey, Sword of Summer,

         Sumarbrander.

JACK

The worst is yet to come, when I'm

  with my new commander.

FREY

      You mean Surt, at *Ragnarok*.

JACK

The Black Onc of Muspellheim.

On the day of doom, he'll wield

  me –

FREY

     – and free the Wolf. Chaos time.

JACK

Boiling seas. Blood-red skies.

FREY

    Gods will vanish. Giants rise.

37

JACK

I'll be sad to see you go.

FREY

Will you really?

JACK

Really? No.

FREY

Destiny is destiny. We all have our
parts to play.

JACK

I'll act mine now then, Nature Boy,
and say, 'See you later, Frey.'

FREY

There'll never be another
quite like you, Sword of Summer.
Our paths may cross again.
If not . . . goodbye, old friend.

FREYA

TYPE: Goddess

HOME WORLD: Originally from Vanaheim, sent to Asgard after the Aesir–Vanir War, now back in Vanaheim

APPEARANCE: Bathed in and emanates golden warmth. Long blonde hair braided in a single thick plait. Lithe figure clad in a white halter top, mid-length skirt and a gold belt. Carries a knife and key ring on the belt.

FAMILY: Daughter of Njord; twin sister of Frey

BEST KNOWN FOR: Presiding over Folkvanger, where half the slain heroes spend their afterlife. Sheds tears of *red gold*. Expert practitioner of alf seidr. Has a passion for love, pleasure and fine dwarven-crafted jewellery. Her signature piece, *Brisingamen*, is a very sparkly ruby-and-diamond lacework necklace of unsurpassed beauty.

MY CHAT WITH FREYA
by Snorri Sturluson

When Helgi scheduled an interview for me with the lovely goddess Freya, I found myself wishing I'd spent more time battling in the fields and less dining on slabs of Saehrimnir. But then I recalled that because I was dead my physique wouldn't change no matter how much I exercised. I settled for spritzing myself liberally with my favourite lady-pleasing cologne, Thane for Men.

I was about to make my way through Yggdrasil to Vanaheim when Thor stopped me, shoved an envelope in my hand and ordered me to deliver it to Freya. Naturally, I was only too happy to help.

With my raven scribe at my side, I arrived in the throne room of Sessrumnir, Freya's mansion, at the appointed hour. Instead of the goddess, however, I found a scruffy-looking individual wearing a multi-hued short-sleeved garment bearing the words KEEP CALM AND FOLKVANGER ON lounging on the dais.

MAN: Whoa, dude, are you supposed to be in here?

SNORRI STURLUSON: Yes. The goddess
Freya herself is to honour me with her presence.

M: Cool. I'm Miles. And, judging by your
body odour [leans close and sniffs SS], I'm
guessing you're a Fart Elf.

SS [indignant]: I am a thane.

M: Sorry, my bad. Well, Athane, I'm not
sure when Freya's going to be home. Can I get
you a beverage item or some salty snackage
while you're waiting?

I was saved from being rude by the arrival of Freya
in her cat-drawn chariot. She was every bit as radiant
as I remembered her. With her was a young woman –
newly deceased, by her bewildered look.

FREYA:
Snorri, darling.
It's been too
long. [Air-kisses
SS.] *Mwah. Mwah.*
Miles, be a love and
take – what was your name again, dear?

WOMAN: Ag-Agnes.

F: Hmm. [Taps finger on lips.] Are you *quite* certain Ag-Agnes is the name you want for the rest of your death?

AG-AGNES: What do you mean *the rest of my death*?

F: Maybe something a little perkier. Let's see. [Strokes cats.] I think *Kitty* will do nicely. That's what we'll call you, my dear.

KITTY: Who are you people?

F: Miles, explain everything to Kitty, will you?

M: I'm on it. [Fires a finger gun at SS.] Catch ya later, Athane. Here, Kitty, Kitty, Kitty!

K: Seriously. What is going on?

F: Oh, darling, don't you see? You're dead.

K: I'm *dead*?

M [grabbing Kitty in a headlock and giving her knuckle noogies]: Come on, Kit-Kat, it's not so bad!

K: I'm *dead*?

[Miles and Kitty depart.]

F: Sweet girl. She makes designer glasses. [Slips on bejeweled cat-eyed spectacles.]

43

When she died, I just knew I had to have her for Folkvanger.

SS: Valhalla's loss, I'm sure. How did she perish?

F: A gas explosion. She died while dragging someone from the fire. Speaking of gas [sniffs SS], you're rather pungent.

SS: Am I?

F: Yes. Do take a step back, dear. My eyes are starting to water red-gold.

SS: My apologies. Before I forget, I have a message for you from Thor.

F [reads Thor's note*]: Oh, Odin's Eye, not again. Snorri, sweetie, we'll have to reschedule. Thor needs to borrow something of mine right away. Can you deliver it to him?

SS: Your wish is my command, my lady. What am I to bring?

F: My magic cloak of falcon feathers. He has to fly to Jotunheim to search for . . . well, I'm not at liberty to say.

---

* Freya tossed the note aside after reading it. The recording raven caught a glimpse of two words: *hammer* and *missing*.

SS: Might I use the cloak to return to Asgard?

F: I'd like nothing better than to allow that.

SS: Wonderful!

F: But no. I'm concerned your odour would negatively affect the feathers. You understand, of course. Carry it at arm's length, will you? Off you go now, there's a love.

As of publication time, my interview with the dazzling goddess had not been rescheduled.

SKIRNIR

TYPE: God

HOME WORLDS: Alfheim and Asgard

APPEARANCE: Nice-looking, if a bit shifty-eyed

BEST KNOWN FOR: Being Frey's servant and messenger. He received the Sword of Summer in exchange for promising that he would convince Gerd, a frost giantess, to marry Frey. He was also sent to the dwarves to instruct them to make the magic rope, *Gleipnir*, that would bind Fenris Wolf.

I SHOULD HAVE KNOWN BETTER . . .

by Skirnir

It's not every day I get my hands on a fine piece of magical weaponry. So, when Frey offered to give me Sumarbrander in exchange for going to Jotunheim to talk to Gerd for him, you'd better believe I said yes.

But there was a catch: the sword was destined to end up in Surt's hands. You heard right. Surt, the Black One, Lord of Muspellheim and, oh, I don't know, the one who brings chaos to the world, was supposed to get *my* blade one day.

When I found out, I was a little anxious about Surt coming after me to get the sword. Then I thought, *Well, he won't come after me if I don't have it on me.*

This is where my good-for-nothing son comes into the story. He'd been moaning about how he was bored in Asgard, how all the other gods got their kids the latest cool stuff, how I never let him go exploring in the other worlds, blah, blah, blah. I'd had it up to here with him, so I decided to send him away. 'Pick where you want to go,' I told him.

First he said Alfheim, then he changed his mind

and said Nidavellir. I was about to send him straight to Ginnungagap when he finally decided on Midgard. 'But I don't want to walk or ride a horse. I want to go on a boat. Not a little boat – a *big* boat, with sails and rowers. And I want to be captain. That way, everybody has to obey me!'

'But you don't know one thing about sailing, especially navigating a Midgard ocean,' I pointed out.

'Why do you have to be such a hater?' he whined. 'You never let me do anything!'

I found him a ship pretty quickly after that. The crew that came with it looked a little sketchy, but what can you do?

And this is where the sword comes back into the story. Besides worrying about Surt showing up to take it, I'd had the blade long enough to know it was never going to feel right in my hands. I couldn't give it back to Frey, because he'd pledged it to me; and I couldn't give it to just anybody, because what if they gave it to Surt?

So I did the only logical thing. I wrapped it in some old blankets and hid it in the hold of the ship. The second my rotten kid was on board, I bellowed 'Bon voyage!' and shoved the vessel away from the dock with my foot. I assumed he wouldn't darken my door again for some time, and, when he did return I'd have figured out what to do about Sumarbrander.

I know what you're thinking: incompetent captain, sketchy crew, magic sword, dangerous ocean, unfamiliar world – what could possibly go wrong?

I found out when my kid came sailing back in on a different ship, complaining about being seasick, about how his crew didn't listen to him and about it not being his fault.

'What wasn't your fault?' I asked, though I was pretty sure I knew the answer.

Surprise, surprise, the boat had sunk off the shore of some Midgard backwater, taking the sword with it. The foolish boy didn't know exactly where the vessel went down – or, if he did, he wasn't saying.

So technically my son is the one who lost the sword. But if you want to pin Sumarbrander's disappearance on me, fine. I'll take the blame for my kid. What else is new?

MIMIR

TYPE: God

HOME WORLD: Originally from Asgard, sent to Vanaheim after the war. Now dwells in the well of knowledge at the roots of Yggdrasil.

APPEARANCE: A wrinkly faced, rusty-haired severed head with a beard and an unfortunate underbite – until properly hydrated. Then a smooth-faced, rusty-haired severed head with a beard and an unfortunate underbite.

BEST KNOWN FOR: Not having a body. Also, letting individuals drink from the well of knowledge in exchange for servitude, unspeakable anguish or both. Runs pachinko parlours when not bobbing about in the waters of infinite wisdom.

TIME ON MY HANDS
by Mimir

There's something I want to get off my chest. I hear what you people say behind my back. You think I'd give my right arm to be the way I was before the Aesir–Vanir war. Not so. Cross my heart, I washed my hands of Asgard and Vanaheim long ago.

Don't get me wrong: life in the well of knowledge isn't a walk in the park. I've learned things that have sent shivers down my spine. And it can be a real pain in the neck when the gods, dwarves, giants, you name it, come to cry on my shoulder. Sometimes I try to give them a leg up, let 'em have a sip in exchange for a little something-something. Other times, though, they're so irritating I just want to give them a knuckle sandwich. Mostly I just cross my fingers that they don't show their faces here again.

But, on the plus side, I've got plenty of elbow room down here in the well. Tons of free time on my hands, too, and I don't just sit around twiddling my thumbs. Nah, instead of dragging my feet, I've invented some stuff. Got my fingers in a lot of pies, actually, and been making money hand over fist, if you want to know the truth. Here are just a few of the creations that took off:

STRAW: Whether sucking up a favourite beverage or shooting a spit-soaked wad of paper at an unsuspecting target, this simple tube can do it all. Straws come in fifty-, one-hundred- and five-hundred-count packages and are available in clear, opaque white, striped, or neon colours. Make 'em bendy or curly for just a little more moola!

BASEBALL CAP: It's the headwear sensation that's sweeping the nations! Versatile enough for use in any world. The brim can protect dwarves from the never-ending Alfheim light and the blinding sun of Midgard. Elves, wear it backwards for a funky street-cred look and let the sun's rays (and admiring raves!) bring you back to life. Choose from a wide variety of colours and brim shapes – or use the patented design tool to customize your own unique style. Adjustable back strap makes it a perfect fit for any head.

PILLOW: You've had a long day. Now it's time to relax. Let us help with our feather-filled rectangle of downy softness, the perfect comfort zone in which to nestle your head for the night. When ordering, please specify falcon, raven, pigeon or eagle fill. Allergic to feathers? Try our all-natural goat-fur alternative instead. Act now and get a second pillow *free*. Shipping and handling charges may apply.

HEL

TYPE: Goddess

HOME WORLD: Helheim

APPEARANCE: One half beautiful woman with elven-pale skin and long dark hair and one half horrifying rotted corpse

FAMILY: The daughter of Loki and a giantess; sister of Fenris Wolf and Jormungand

BEST KNOWN FOR: Ruling Helheim, the land of the dishonourable dead

EVITE FROM HEL

You're Invited to Our Family Reunion!

My, how time flies! It seems like an eternity since we've all got together. If you agree it's been too long, join me here in Helheim to swap stories, share milestones, reminisce about the old days and talk about the future!

Please bring a dish and a beverage to share. Hope to see you in Helheim!

When: Nine days hence

Where: Helheim

RSVP: By next Frigg's Day

PS: Dress warm – it can get a bit chilly here in the underworld!

Invitee/Relationship to Host	Attending: Yes/No/Maybe	Message to Host
Loki/Father	Maybe	I'm a little tied up right now, but I'll see if I can break free.
Angrboda/Mother	Yes	A thousand years, and not so much as a card or a call from you, Fenny or Jor. I don't know why I'm surprised. I'm only your mother. Why should my needs be your concern? You're ashamed of me because I'm a giantess. That's it, isn't it? I don't think you really want me to come. I mean, why else would you invite Sigyn and Sleipnir? You know how I feel about them. Fine. I'll come. But I won't have fun.
Fenris Wolf/Brother	No	Would have attended if Odin was on the menu
Jormungand/Brother	Mmmphhmmm	(Note from Host: Jor left a voice mail, but I couldn't understand it, probably because he had his tail in his mouth again. Crossing fingers he shows up with his famous sushi!)
Sigyn/Stepmother	Yes	I should stay at my poor husband Loki's side to keep the venom from hitting his face, but I'll be there. Ooo! I'll bring baby pictures of Narvi and Vali!
Narvi/Stepbrother	No	Deceased (torn to shreds by Vali after Vali was turned into a wolf)
Vali/Stepbrother	No	Deceased (disembowelled after tearing Narvi to shreds)
Sleipnir/Step-horse	Yes	Bummed my mom Loki's not coming, but I'll trot on by! Let me know if I can bring my boy Stanley – he wants to meet the other side of the family!

HEIMDALL

TYPE: God

HOME WORLD: Asgard

APPEARANCE: Big, beefy, horn-toting, far-seeing and somewhat sleep-deprived. Has gold teeth.

FAMILY: Born of the Nine Mothers. (Don't ask me. It's his story to tell.)

BEST KNOWN FOR: Standing guarding over the Bifrost, the rainbow bridge that connects Asgard and Midgard

TESTING, TESTING

Don't be surprised if you hear this over the hotel loudspeaker one day:

BLAA! BLAA! BLAA!

Attention! This is a test of the Asgard Emergency Broadcast System. For the next sixty seconds, *Heimdall* will blow his horn. This sound will one day herald the coming of Ragnarok. If this were the actual day of doom, you would be informed that Heimdall had sighted the giants amassing outside Asgard's fortifications and at the far end of the rainbow bridge. Instructions for defending Asgard against their murderous rampage would follow.

This is only a test.

BLAAAAAAAAAAAAAAAAAAAAAAAAAAAAAAAAA AAAAAAAAAAAAAAAAAA!

This concludes the test of the Asgard Emergency Broadcast System. We now return you to your regularly scheduled existence.

RAN

TYPE: Goddess

HOME WORLD: The sea

APPEARANCE: Ancient-looking, with wrinkly pale white skin, cloudy green eyes and blonde hair streaked with grey. Wears a one-of-a-kind silver net skirt encrusted with random objects and the souls of those lost at sea.

FAMILY: Married to *Aegir*, lord of the waves; they have nine daughters

BEST KNOWN FOR: Scavenging and hoarding assorted flotsam from the ocean

FINDERS KEEPERS
by Ran

One day long, long ago, I was having a lovely drift on my husband Aegir's waves when something snagged on my skirt. It looked like a long, skinny wooden bowl – a *boat*, Njord, the god of ships and stuff, called it. When I turned it over, a handful of humans fell out and started drowning.

Out of nowhere, a flock of Odin's *Valkyries* swarmed the sky. Then Njord's daughter – what's-her-name, the pretty one – Freya? Freya flew in on her feline-fuelled chariot. Hel made an appearance, too, rumbling up from below. They circled the humans, checking them out and arguing over who should get which of the very nearly newly deceased. It was like a shark's feeding frenzy for souls.

Now, I never intended to host an afterlife. But, the way I saw it, the sea was *my* turf, so those souls were *mine*. I caught them in my skirt and held on tight.

The Valkyries pretended they didn't want them anyway – not heroic enough for Valhalla, they claimed – and left. Freya laughed at me and then made off with some sparkly bits the humans had stored in a chest. From then on, I made sure to grab any sparkly bits I found, just to spite her.

Hel gave me the most grief. She complained that Odin and Freya always got the pick of the litter, so she should at least get everyone else. I made my point about there being different rules in international waters, etc. I also threatened to sic her brother the World Serpent on her if she didn't leave immediately. Jormungand and I have an understanding, so I knew he'd come through for me if I asked. In the end, Hel agreed that anyone lost at sea would remain with me forever. So I won that battle.

Best of all? Njord let me keep the boat for my collection. Want to see it?

FRIGG

TYPE: Goddess

HOME WORLD: Asgard

APPEARANCE: Beautiful and self-assured with a
touch of sadness

FAMILY: Wife of Odin, mother of Balder and *Hod*

BEST KNOWN FOR: Being the goddess of marriage,
motherhood and relationships. She's also the queen
of Asgard.

BALDER

TYPE: God

HOME WORLD: Originally from Asgard, now doomed to Helheim for eternity

APPEARANCE: Incredibly handsome

FAMILY: Son of Odin and Frigg; brother of Hod

BEST KNOWN FOR: Being killed by Hod's mistletoe arrow (but it wasn't his fault!)

HOD

TYPE: God

HOME WORLD: Asgard

APPEARANCE: Good looking and blind

FAMILY: Son of Odin and Frigg; brother of Balder

BEST KNOWN FOR: Being tricked by Loki into killing Balder with an arrowhead made of mistletoe

---

IDUN

TYPE: Goddess

HOME WORLD: Asgard

APPEARANCE: Youthful, pretty

BEST KNOWN FOR: Being the keeper of the apples of immortality. Also for being kidnapped by and rescued from the giant *Thjazi*.

HONIR

TYPE: God

HOME WORLD: Originally from Asgard, sent to Vanaheim after the Aesir–Vanir war

APPEARANCE: Has a constantly confused expression on his handsome face

BEST KNOWN FOR: Irritating the Vanir gods so much with his indecisiveness that they decapitated Mimir

DEAR FRIGG
A Weekly Advice Column

Dear Frigg:

I am the mother of two wonderful boys. My problem isn't with them but with a third boy they met at school. It seems every time they're together this third boy coaxes my younger son into playing a prank on my older boy. While the pranks have been harmless, I'm wondering if I should intervene before things get too out of hand. Or should I just let boys be boys?

Signed,
Three's a Crowd

Dear Three's:

For the love of Odin, learn from my example and intervene! Like you, I have two sons, Hod and Balder. Growing up, Balder was the best of the best — handsome, kind, cheerful, brave, generous and tidy — and everybody, including Hod, loved him. He looked out for Hod, because Hod was blind and because he loved him.

All would have been fine had my boys not started hanging out with another boy, named Loki. Loki pretended to be their friend — but he secretly despised Balder, so whenever he had the chance he tried to hurt him. But Balder was safe, for when he was a child I asked everything in the world not to hurt him. Everything agreed, and so Balder was invulnerable.

Or so we all thought.

Sadly, I overlooked one tiny plant: mistletoe. Loki used my oversight to his advantage. He fashioned an arrowhead of mistletoe and convinced Hod, who trusted him, to shoot it. Hod didn't realize he was aiming at his brother. The mistletoe missile hit Balder and . . . well, Balder has been in Helheim ever since. He could have made it back to me if it weren't for Hel's unreasonableness. But that's another story.

So yes, you could 'just let boys be boys'. But ask yourself: is it worth the risk?

Sincerely,
Frigg

Dear Frigg:

I like a girl, but she doesn't like me. I'm thinking of asking this other boy who owes me a favour to see if he can make her go out with me. Do you think that's a good idea?

Signed,
Pining

Dear Pining:

It's terrible to be in love when the object of your affection doesn't reciprocate. But the truth is, you can't 'make' a girl go out with you, and you certainly shouldn't try.

I remember when a boy named Loki tricked my friend Idun into going on a date with a giant bully named Thjazi. Idun never would have gone out with Thjazi if he'd asked her himself. In fact, when she realized who the date was with, she felt totally trapped. Is that how you want your special girl to feel? I sincerely hope not!

Still tempted to pursue your plan? Maybe you won't be when you hear how Idun's story ended. While suffering through the date, she managed to send word of her predicament to her warrior friends. She had lots of friends, and not just because she gives out apples of immortality. Anyway, they came storming to her rescue. Once she was safe, they turned up the heat on Thjazi and made sure he would never treat a girl — or anyone else, for that matter — with such disrespect again.

So I urge you, Pining, to think twice before you move forward. Remember, your girl probably has friends, too.

Sincerely,
Frigg

DEAR FRIGG:

MY COWORKER AND I ARE HAVING A DISAGREEMENT. WE DO ALL THE WORK, AND OUR BOSS TAKES ALL THE CREDIT. I'M SICK AND TIRED OF IT. I SAY WE SHOULD STOP WORKING AND LET HIM TAKE THE BLAME, BUT MY COWORKER SAYS THAT WILL END BADLY FOR US. WHAT DO YOU THINK WE SHOULD DO?

SIGNED,
FRUSTRATED

Dear Frustrated:

Your situation reminds me of two friends, Mimir and Honir, who were chosen for an exchange programme to another land. People there loved Honir, because he was good-looking. They believed he was smart, so they came to him for advice, which he gave willingly. What the people didn't know was that Honir was as dumb as rocks. It was Mimir, highly intelligent but lacking in charisma, who was feeding Honir the solutions to their problems.

This system worked fine until Mimir got fed up and stopped helping Honir. When Honir's advice suddenly went downhill, the people realized they had been duped. They raged at Honir. The simpleton explained it had all been Mimir's idea. So they went after Mimir and . . . well, let's just say he ended up in deep water and leave it at that.

So before you lose your head over this, I advise you to consider your situation carefully. Will your boss really end up bearing the blame? Or will he point the finger at you?

Sincerely,
Frigg

TYR

TYPE: God

HOME WORLD: Asgard

APPEARANCE: A one-handed warrior

BEST KNOWN FOR: Having his hand eaten by Fenris Wolf while the other gods bound the beast with the rope Gleipnir

OUCH!
by Tyr

Hey, kids! Here's an important safety tip from your old Uncle *Tyr*! Don't insert your hand inside a wolf's mouth – or a lion's, bear's, alligator's or crocodile's mouth, or in a lawn mower, garbage disposal, snowblower or blender – because, if you do, you're not going to have that hand for much longer! Don't believe me? Ask my good friend Captain Hook how he got his name! And remember: gloves and mittens come in pairs for a reason!

ULLER

TYPE: God

HOME WORLD: Asgard

APPEARANCE: Disgruntled backwoodsman

BEST KNOWN FOR: Claims he invented archery, snowshoes and other winter sports equipment

Dear Mr *Uller*:

We have received your recent letter outlining your continued assertion that items you invented are being manufactured and sold in our country – referred to by you as Midgard – without your permission. These inventions include the following:

Skis (alpine and Nordic)

Ice skates (hockey and figure)

Snowboards

Snowshoes

Sleighs

Sleds (runner and flat-bottomed)

The sport of archery

As we have stated in previous correspondence, unless you can provide evidence that you are indeed the patent rights holder for these inventions, we cannot pursue the matter through legal channels. Please note that your sworn statement that you are 'the god of these things' will not be deemed sufficient by the court. Unless you can offer more substantial documentation, we must consider this matter closed once and for all, and respectfully ask that you do not contact these offices again.

Sincerely,

James Lovasock,
Attorney-at-Law

NJORD

TYPE: God

HOME WORLD: Originally from Vanaheim, sent to Asgard after the Aesir–Vanir War

APPEARANCE: Like a classic fisherman, complete with yellow slicker, pipe, thick woollen sweater and weather-beaten face

FAMILY: Father of twins Frey and Freya

BEST KNOWN FOR: Being the god of ships, sailors and fishermen

MYTHICAL BEINGS

by Hunding

Surprise, surprise, Helgi's insisting I introduce you to this group, too. One of these days, I swear I'll . . . Never mind.

I'm using the term *mythical* for the benefit of you once-human einherjar, by the way. There's nothing made-up or imaginary about these beings. They're real. The sooner you believe in their existence, the safer you'll be. Maybe.

First up, the jotun, or giants. They come in all sizes, not just enormous. Species include stone, frost, fire and shape-shifting. Many live in Jotunheim; others dwell in Muspellheim and Niflheim. Some are strong. Some are clever. Some are masters of illusion.

But almost all of them have a mean streak as wide as the Bifrost bridge. They can sometimes be swayed to work with you, but never count on them being your ally. And I mean never *ever*.

Next, elves. They are tall, handsome beings who thrive in light and hate darkness. They used to be into alf seidr, or elf magic, and the study of runes. Now most of them are into sitting around and surfing the Internet or watching their favourite programmes on Alflix. Word of warning: elves are all about beauty. If you aren't one of the beautiful people . . . well, it's best you avoid Alfheim. In their own way, elves can be almost as cut-throat as giants.

Characterizing dwarves is a little trickier. There's one kind called *svartalf*, which means 'dark elf.' Why isn't a svartalf an elf? Don't ask me. I didn't create them. It's said the svartalfs are taller and more attractive than your average dwarf because they are descended from Freya, but I can't say for certain. Any dwarf that isn't a svartalf is just a regular old dwarf. All dwarves, by the way, were originally maggots. The gods saw them crawling around in Ymir's flesh, from which the world was created, and the gods decided, *Hey, let's turn those maggots into sentient beings!* Ever since, the dwarves have been tunnelling through the dark places of the earth and avoiding the light. I wouldn't bring up the maggot story while you're travelling in Nidavellir, though, unless you want to start a fight.

Valkyries you already know about, since you're in Valhalla, but there's an entry for them anyway. If I didn't include them, they would get mad, and I try to avoid making shield maidens angry.

Finally, there are the Norns. These eerie ladies are tapped into everyone's destinies. You have to experience them to get the full picture. Though, come to think of it, the experience is just as tough to fathom as the Norns themselves. Best to do what the rest of us do, which is pray you never have dealings with them. Trust me, it's just easier that way.

That about covers the main categories. But be aware that you could encounter other beings who may strive to deceive, distract or manipulate. They go by the names *draugr* (zombies), *vala* (seers), *witches* (witches) and *telemarketers* (annoyances).

THE GIANTS

SURT

TYPE: Fire

HOME WORLD: Muspellheim

APPEARANCE: Unbelievably handsome, evil and well dressed. All black – hair, clothes, skin – except for mesmerizing red eyes.

BEST KNOWN FOR: Undying interest in unleashing the start of Ragnarok by freeing Fenris Wolf with the Sword of Summer.

Editor's Warning: The following entry contains disturbing content. Repeated attempts have been made to delete it, but due to magic beyond our control, it remains permanently typeset onto these pages. We urge you to skip it. If you do choose to read it, please be aware that the Hotel Valhalla and its employees cannot be held accountable for your emotional well-being.

YOUR DOOM
by Surt

Einherjar, hear this from my own lips:

You train in vain. Destiny decrees that come Ragnarok I will free Fenris Wolf with the blade known as Sumarbrander. The Wolf will devour Odin and then open his jaws to consume these worlds. My army of giants and I will overwhelm Heimdall and storm over the Bifrost. We will destroy everything in our path in the all-consuming fire of chaos.

You will die. Humans will die. Dwarves will die. Elves will die. Gods and goddesses and all creatures, save giants, will die.

So battle each morn knowing that my kind will reign supreme in the end. Resurrect each afternoon knowing that we will re-create the cosmos for giants alone. Feast each evening knowing that we will dine in triumph over your corpses. Slumber each night knowing that your doom is foreordained.

Ragnarok. It is your end and our beginning.

Burn!

BURN! HA-HA-HA-HA-HA-HA!

Also . . . burn.

YMIR

TYPE: MASSIVE

HOME WORLD: He is literally every part of Midgard

APPEARANCE: Before he was killed by Odin and company, he was gigantic. Afterwards, not so much.

BEST KNOWN FOR: Being sliced and diced by Odin and his brothers, who used his body parts to make Midgard

GREETINGS FROM GINNUNGAGAP

by Ymir

Hunding stole my story. I won't go to pieces over that. (Ha! *Ba-boom, shish!* Gods, I love a good punchline. Too bad that wasn't one! Ha!)

Instead, I'll tell you about the cow, Audhumbla. She was in the Gap with me. And she was big. (*How big was she?*) That cow was so big that when she sat around the Gap she really sat around the Gap!

Seriously, though, Audhumbla the cow kept me alive right up to the moment Odin and his brothers killed me. Why they didn't go for the cow, I'll never know. Udderly ridiculous, am I right? (Ha!)

I would have paid Odin to kill that cow, actually. Why? While I was alive, she started in on this big salt lick. Show of hands: who here has ever listened to an enormous bovine with a really wet tongue lick something for months? No one? Consider yourselves lucky. Lick, lick, lick, lick, day and night, night and day. It sounded as if someone was mixing up a tub of tuna and mayo right by my ear. Drove me nuts until I was like, *Kill me now!*

Turns out the licking *did* kill me. After . . . I don't know, *forever*, the cow's tongue uncovered a god hidden in the salt. This god,  Buri, had a son named Borr. Borr married my grand-daughter Bestla – that's right, I had kids and grandkids, none of your business how – and Bestla and Borr had Odin, Vili and Ve, who . . . well, you know the rest. Chop, chop, slice and dice, so long, Ymir.

The joke's on them, though, isn't it? Because my side of the family, the giants – they're going to have the last laugh when they lick the gods in the battle to end all battles.

UTGARD-LOKI

TYPE: Shape-shifter

HOME WORLD: Jotunheim

APPEARANCE: Before eating one of Idun's apples of immortality, he was an old man with grey hair; afterwards, he was a young man with black hair. Wears boots, leather breeches, an eagle-feather tunic and one golden armband embellished with bloodstones.

BEST KNOWN FOR: Shape-shifting and powerful sorcery. Also, king of the mountain giants and therefore future enemy of the gods and einherjar.

GUESS WHO?

by Snorri Sturluson

A short time after my conversation with the lady Freya was interrupted, I received an invitation to join her on the outskirts of Jotunheim. Although I was surprised by the choice of location, I hastened there, since it was not for me to question a goddess. I arrived to find her in high spirits.

SNORRI STURLUSON: My lady Freya, I thank you for seeing me again so soon. You are, as always, a picture of loveliness.

FREYA: Why, thank you, Snorri. I could just kiss you for that. In fact, I think I will. [Kisses SS right on the lips.] *Mmmmmmmwah!*

SS [surprised]: M-my lady! Words fail me!

F: That's a first.

SS: Er . . .

F: Hold that thought. I have another surprise for you! [Air shimmers. The goddess is replaced by a massive giant.] Ta-da!

SS [shrieks]: *Aaaaaaugh!*

UTGARD-LOKI [doubling over with laughter]: The look on your face! Priceless! I'm telling you, Snorts, you einherjar are so gullible. Reminds me of the pranks I played on Thor all those years ago. You know what I'm talking about, right?

SS: I couldn't say.

U-L: I could. The great Thunder God comes waltzing into my territory to challenge my posse to feats of strength and awesomeness. The first night he's here, know what he does? Camps out in a giant's *glove*, thinking it's a *house*! A *glove*! But that's not all. Want to hear what happens next?

SS: Do I have a choice?

U-L: No. The next morning, Thor tries to brain a sleeping giant with his famous hammer. The giant wakes up and asks if a leaf landed on him. Giant goes back to sleep. Thor whacks him again. Giant wakes up and says he felt an acorn bounce on his forehead. Third time, the giant wonders if the hammer hit is a plop of bird poop. [Leans in.] Guess who the giant was.

SS: You.

U-L: Me!

SS: Hilarious. [Stands.] Now if you'll excuse me –

U-L: Sit.

SS: Right. [Sits hurriedly.]

U-L: So now, Thor comes sauntering into my castle bragging about how great he is. I say, 'Go on, then, prove it. First, drink everything in this cup. Second, pick up my grey cat. Finally, wrestle that wizened old crone over there to the ground.' [Leans in.] Want to know a secret?

SS: You used sorcery so Thor couldn't win.

U-L [guffawing]: I used sorcery so Thor couldn't win! The cup was actually the ocean. The cat was Jormungand, on loan from Aegir's realm. And the crone was old age itself. No one can beat old age, Snorts!

SS: Not even a god? Or what about Idun and her apples of immortality?

U-L [frowning dangerously]: Don't bring up that lady around me, Snorts. She did one of my guys wrong.

SS: Like Loki, my lips are sealed.

U-L: You ain't half bad, thane. Maybe I'll even spare you at Ragnarok. But probably not.

[At this time, a pigeon delivers a message to *Utgard-Loki*.]

U-L [reading and grinning]: Oh, I'm loving this! Listen, Snorts, I gotta get going. Just heard a certain someone thinks a certain missing item is buried here in Jotunheim. He's digging holes all over the place looking for it. This I gotta see. [Turns into an eagle and flies off.]

I later learned that the someone was Thor and the item was Mjolnir. Rumour has it the hammer was, indeed, in Jotunheim, but Thor had yet to discover its whereabouts.

GERD

TYPE: Frost

HOME WORLD: Niflheim

APPEARANCE: Large and beautiful, with glowing arms

BEST KNOWN FOR: Being irresistible to Frey, the god of spring and summer

GERD JUST WANTS
TO BE HEARD
by Gerd

People say I'm a stick in the mud.
I just like feeling the cold earth under my toes.
Don't need to dress up
Or go anywhere but my front yard.

Can I help it if my skin glows?
It has attracted ships, birds
And the unwanted attention
Of gods from afar.

Frey couldn't even ask me himself.
Sent his servant to propose.
Tried to woo me with golden apples,
But I like the red kind better.

When the fancy ring didn't work either,
Skirnir got angry
And pulled out that talking sword.
My words didn't matter any more.

I married Frey, and we've made it work.
He's all about nature and love.
Still, sometimes, I can't help but wish
I could crank up the air conditioner.

ELVES

HOME WORLD: Alfheim

APPEARANCE: Tall, good-looking, pale skin; will die without sunlight

BEST KNOWN FOR: Being one-time experts at archery and alf seidr, and occasionally decoding the mysteries of runes. Now mostly experts at video viewing.

ALF SEIDR MAKING
A COMEBACK

A special report compiled by the staff of *Alfheim Today Online: All the News That's Fit to View.*

ALFHEIM – It appears that alf seidr – the magic power that fell out of favour with the rise of technology – is getting a new toehold in Alfheim. And not everyone is happy about it.

'We abandoned that magic for a reason,' stated Smokescreen, owner and chief elf operator of ElfVision Communications. 'It's a health hazard. It demands too much from its practitioners. I've heard some even perish attempting to learn the simplest spells! Trust me – if you want a truly magical experience, stick to twenty-four-hour streaming video. All you need for that is a comfortable couch, an enormous monitor connected to ElfVision and a handy remote – not self-sacrifice.'

The risk to alf seidr practitioners is very real. Performing feats such as healing wounds and issuing defensive power bursts requires a massive output of life-force energy. Expending that energy can leave one drained for hours, even days, according to witnesses.

'I had a case where an elf used alf seidr to help a friend who was having a severe allergic reaction,' one concerned doctor told *Alfheim Today*. 'She saved her friend but almost killed herself in the process.'

The biggest threat to life and limb comes from attempting to understand runestones. These symbols embody the essence of the universe. Channelling that essence has been known to overload one's system and lead to disastrous results, such as death.

Despite the dangers, a grassroots alf seidr movement known as Turn Off and Tune In is steadily gaining momentum, particularly with younger elves. 'They feel disconnected from their parents' sedentary way of life,' stated the head of the movement, Aloe Vera. 'They're curious about the potential of this long-forgotten power. You'll see many of these same elves studying archery, too. Most instructors are from older generations. Seeing the younger set learning from the older ones – it's really inspiring.'

Aloe Vera claims that they don't actively recruit new members. So why have their numbers increased so significantly as of late? 'No doubt the looming threat of Ragnarok has something to do with it,' she admitted. 'They're joining because they believe magic and arrows have a better chance of defeating giants than Wi-Fi and decorative throw pillows.'

Only time will tell if she's right. Until then, the use of alf seidr remains controversial.

DWARVES

HOME WORLD: Nidavellir

APPEARANCE: Craggy and short; will turn to stone if left in the sun too long

BEST KNOWN FOR: Expert metalwork and craftsmanship

METAL IN MOTION
by Gonda

Long before I made barstools for Nabbi's Tavern, I had a career crafting labour-saving devices. You know the type of thing – push a button, pull a lever, turn a knob and ta-da! A machine does your work for you. That career turned out to be unbelievably boring.

Fortunately, destiny steered me in another direction. On an accidental trip to Midgard, I met a human named Rube Goldberg. Goldberg, son of Hannah, came up with these crazy contraptions designed to do simple tasks in the most unnecessarily complicated manner possible. The contraptions, known as Rube Goldberg machines, were poetry in motion.

I took Rube's concept, ran with it straight back to Nidavellir and set about making my own creations. I repurposed bits and pieces I'd salvaged over the years – a fan, a toy truck and a pack of dominoes from Midgard, several cat-food cans from Vanaheim ('Freya's cats ask for it by name!'), a snow shovel from

Niflheim, a coat hanger from my friend Blitzen – you get the idea. I welded and soldered, hammered and fired those pieces into a sequence of interconnected parts. Altogether, they formed a thing of beauty.

My first Rube Goldberg machine was designed to light my kiln. Here's how it worked: a handcrafted silver ball spiralled down a hammered steel track suspended by spun wire from my ceiling. The ball landed in a buffed-to-mirror-shine cat-food can. The can tipped the ball into another can, which tipped it into another and so on through seven cans. The final can tipped the ball into the bed of the toy truck. The truck, refitted for a monorail I'd constructed, shot across the floor and tapped the first in a long twisting line of dominoes that spelled out GONDA. The last falling dominoes climbed up a set of stairs engraved with images of famous dwarves. The final domino struck the coat hanger, now fortified with an enamel finish, sending it whirling around. The coat hanger flicked a switch that turned on the fan. The fan blew against the snow shovel blade. The shovel fell over and landed on the high end of a seesaw that I had forged myself from bronze and decorated with gemstones. The low end flew up and launched another ball – gold this time – clear across the room, where it hit a hammer handed down to me by my ancestors. The hammer fell onto the button that starts my kiln and – voila! The fire lit!

Would it have been easier just to push the button myself? Of course. Would pushing the button have been as satisfying? No way. You might think I'm crazy for spending so much time and effort on such creations. But, to me, metal that moves, moves me.

VALKYRIES

HOME WORLDS: Midgard and Asgard

APPEARANCE: Fierce, strong human females, often on horses. Capable of flight. Armed with shields and swords or axes.

BEST KNOWN FOR: Identifying individuals who have died in the act of saving others and conveying these heroes to Valhalla

FIRST FLIGHT OF A VALKYRIE

Diary Entries [Name withheld to protect author's privacy]

Day One:

I'm a Valkyrie. Man, even after writing it down, it doesn't seem possible! But it's true. I'm an honest-to-goodness Chooser of the Slain, a shield maiden of Odin! One minute, I'm walking down the street. The next, this fierce-looking, helmet-wearing, spear-carrying woman on a flying horse appears in the sky above me. She swoops down and holds out her hand. 'I am Gunilla, captain of the Valkyries,' she says, all serious and imposing. 'You have been chosen by Odin to select and care for fallen heroes in the afterlife, where they will ceaselessly train for Ragnarok, the doomsday battle of the gods against the giants. Do you accept?'

I'd never even heard of Odin or any of those other things, but refusing didn't seem like an option. So here I am in the lobby of Hotel Valhalla with other new recruits, waiting to find out what happens next.

Day Two:

Exhausted. More tomorrow.

Day Five:

Sorry not to have written for a few days. Here's a quick recap of what I've been doing:

- Toured all 540 floors of Hotel Valhalla. Flirted with some good-looking guys on the lower levels.
- Endured a lecture on the Nine Worlds given by some fossilized thane named Snorti. (Might be Snorri? So boring, I almost started *snorri-ing* . . .)
- Had it drilled into my head that we bring back only the immortal essence (i.e. the souls) and leave the bodies of the fallen behind.
- Got fitted for my Valkyrie uniform: helmet, chain-mail tunic, leggings, boots, sword. (Not to brag, but I look smokin' hot as a Viking warrior.)
- Waited on tables in the Feast Hall of the Slain. Einherjar – the proper name of the dead heroes who live (live?) in Valhalla – eat and drink a *lot*.
- Magically returned to Midgard (the human realm, according to Snorti) every dawn to live the days as a normal teenager.

106

I'm due back in Midgard in a few hours. Gotta grab some sleep before then, so goodnight.

PS: Just remembered all the good-looking guys here are dead. Bummer.

Day Nine:

Best. Day. *Ever!*

It started with Gunilla summoning us newbies from Midgard. I was at school, heading to maths class, so I veered into the restroom and climbed out of the window. There was a *whoosh*, and suddenly I was back at the hotel. Don't ask me how. I have no clue.

We gathered in the Feast Hall. It was hours before dinner, so the place was deserted. Gunilla started talking.

'Take a look at the trainees next to you. And know this: one will perish in the line of duty. Just because you can travel to and from this afterlife doesn't mean you're invincible. You can be killed. Die honourably, and your memory will live on forever. Die dishonourably, and you will be forgotten.'

I was thinking, *Okay, might have been nice to know this before I signed up*, when a bunch of veteran Valkyries came in. One approached me, introduced herself as Margaret and said, 'You're going to love what comes next.'

Before I could ask what she meant, Gunilla called out, 'Flight attendants, prepare for takeoff.'

Margaret grabbed my arm and said, 'Don't look down.' Then she shot straight up into the air! Here's the good part: *I went with her! I. Was. Flying!*

Okay, sure, technically, *I* didn't fly. Margaret did, with me Velcroed to her for dear life. But, oh my Odin, it was still amazing. Tomorrow, I get to try it myself. It's going to be *awesome*!

Day Ten:

Hour one: Took off. Crashed into Laeradr (stupid tree). Took off. Fell onto the thanes' table. Took off. Crashed into Laeradr and then fell onto the thanes' table. An unbelievably fat tree-dwelling goat landed on top of me.

Hour three: re-enacted the Wright brothers' first flight at Kitty Hawk. That is, got airborne for less than a minute before inevitably crashing (into Laeradr yet again).

Hour six: longer flight. Landed on my feet! (I immediately fell on my face, but still . . . result!)

Hour nine: actual swooping and soaring occurred! Sound the horn of triumph, people! I am a Valkyrie!

Day Eleven:

Turns out I have to learn how to fly on a horse made of mist, too. Flying solo with fallen heroes doesn't work so well; apparently they tend to squirm, which causes turbulence. Lessons start tomorrow.

Square one, here I come.

THE NORNS

HOME WORLD: Asgard; specifically, the lake at the roots of the *Tree of Laeradr* in the Feast Hall of the Slain

APPEARANCE: A trio of nine-foot-tall, snow-white, fog-enshrouded, spooky-looking females in flowing white hooded dresses

BEST KNOWN FOR: Controlling the destinies of mortals and gods. Also making enigmatic proclamations about those destinies.

FUN WITH FATE!

We at Hotel Valhalla understand that hearing a proclamation about your destiny can be overwhelming for a new einherji – especially if that proclamation is from the Norns. Why not take a break with Destiny Buzzword? It's easy, fun and sometimes even accurate. To come up with your three key destiny words, find the first letter of your first name, last letter of your last name and the month you were born. For example, Snorri Sturluson was born in March, so his buzzwords are Intelligent, Clever and Coward. Who knows? Maybe someday your words will be revealed to have deep meaning!

DESTINY BUZZWORD

A: Terrible	N: Clever	JAN: Magic
B: Hero	O: Sword	FEB: Betrayal
C: Fight	P: Fearless	MAR: Coward
D: Everlasting	Q: Doomed	APR: Daring
E: Wolf	R: Battle	MAY: Honourable
F: Creative	S: Intelligent	JUN: Victorious
G: Warrior	T: Mistake	JUL: Injury
H: Challenge	U: Quest	AUG: Eviscerate
I: Deadly	V: Ruin	SEP: Darkness
J: Fearsome	W: Sacrifice	OCT: Unlimited
K: Knowledge	X: Search	NOV: Giant
L: Fall	Y: Healer	DEC: Love
M: Worthy	Z: Destroy	

FANTASTIC CREATURES

by Hunding

Now I'm supposed to profile the creatures that can't speak for themselves, as well as those that can but say either incredibly annoying or unbelievably hurtful things. (There are a few hurtful things I'd like to say to Helgi about now . . . I'm leaving this in to see if he even reads my work.)

Our menagerie of beasts fall into three categories: notable, regrettable and edible. Notable ones make worthwhile contributions to the worlds or are significant for other reasons. Those that are regrettable are alarming in every possible way – some more so than others. As for the edible creatures, well, I think that category is self-explanatory.

NIDHOGG

CATEGORY: Regrettable

HOME WORLD: Roots of Yggdrasil

APPEARANCE: Snaky, with sharp teeth and an irritated expression

BEST KNOWN FOR: Gnawing on Yggdrasil's roots

This fearsome dragon has one purpose in life: to cause destruction by eating away at the base of our existence. It's a mystery to me why we put up with this behaviour. I mean, can't someone slip him a chew toy? The only time *Nidhogg* isn't snacking on the roots is when he's coming up with new insults to be delivered to the unnamed resident at the top of the tree.

THE ANONYMOUS EAGLE
OF YGGDRASIL

CATEGORY: Regrettable

HOME WORLD: Top of Yggdrasil

APPEARANCE: Fierce and feathery

BEST KNOWN FOR: Shaking the treetops to cause high winds, earthquakes and storms

This is the aforementioned unnamed resident, i.e. the receiver of Nidhogg's insults. Which brings up a second mystery: why doesn't this bird have a name? If it's a question of selecting one, we could just hold a contest, pick a name out of a helmet, or throw a dart at choices tacked to a board. Seriously, what's the big deal?

Incidentally, the eagle fires insults, along with nasty lies, rumours and other hateful whisperings, right back at Nidhogg. How, you may wonder, are such messages exchanged when the eagle and dragon are at opposite ends of the World Tree? Read on.

RATATOSK

CATEGORY: Very, very regrettable

HOME WORLD: Branches of Yggdrasil

APPEARANCE: An enormous, ferocious red-furred squirrel with yellow eyes and razor-sharp teeth and claws

BEST KNOWN FOR: Carrying insults between the anonymous eagle and Nidhogg. Also, draining the will to live from those who hear its insult-filled *YARK*.

JUST BETWEEN YOU AND ME
by Ratatosk

Come here *(you're slow)*. Don't worry *(anxiety is your middle name)*. I won't bark at you. I want to tell you *(your teammates blame you for that loss)* a secret. I know why Nidhogg and the eagle *(they're laughing at you, not with you)* began trading insults. I know *(your best will never be good enough)*, because I'm the one who started the feud. I was bored *(your stories make everyone yawn)*. To liven things up I sent a whispered taunt *(you've never had an original idea)* down Yggdrasil's trunk to the dragon *(only worms are lowlier than you)* and another up to the eagle *(you'll never fly)*. Care to hear *(you crack under pressure)* what those insults were? Then come closer still *(you're afraid of everything and everyone)* and let me whisper *(you're too trusting)* in your ear *(you have earwax)*.

YAAAARK!

HEIDRUN

CATEGORY: Edible (sort of)

HOME WORLD: Asgard; specifically, the branches of Laeradr in the Hotel Valhalla

APPEARANCE: Overweight, leaky goat

BEST KNOWN FOR: Providing milk that is brewed into mead

EIKTHRYMIR
(ALSO GOES BY THE NICKNAME 'IKE')

CATEGORY: Notable

HOME WORLD: Asgard, specifically the branches of Laeradr

APPEARANCE: Stag with water-gushing antlers

BEST KNOWN FOR: Spouting water for the rivers and streams of the world

SAEHRIMNIR

CATEGORY: Edible

HOME WORLD: Asgard, specifically the Feast Hall of the Slain in the Hotel Valhalla

APPEARANCE: Enormous animal of indeterminate species

BEST KNOWN FOR: Being the main course at dinner every night for every resident

A TRICKSTER TRAITOR
by Halfborn Gunderson

This story was told to me by one of the older einherjar, who heard it from someone else who used to catch Heidrun's milk in the cauldron, who claims to have heard it from Heidrun herself. Whether it is true or not, I cannot say, but neither can I imagine a reason for the goat to make up such a tale. In the end, you must judge for yourself.

One night Ike and Heidrun were hanging out with Saehrimnir, keeping him company while he resurrected, as they often did, when the subject of Ragnarok came up.

'It occurs to me,' Heidrun said, shifting slightly so her milk wouldn't keep dripping onto Saehrimnir's flank, 'that no one has ever mentioned what our fate is to be when the giants re-create the cosmos.'

'I imagine we'd be useful to the jotun,' Saehrimnir mused. 'After all, they'll need water and mead and food, won't they?'

'I don't know. Who can tell with giants?' Heidrun said. 'What do you think, Ike?'

'We could always ask the Norns if our destinies are to die with the gods or live with the giants,' the stag replied. The threesome cast anxious looks at the lake below. 'Or not,' Ike added.

'Maybe I can help.' Loki swung down from a branch above and landed beside Saehrimnir. In the days before he was tied to a boulder, he often hid in Laeradr, because it was a useful spot from which to spy on the other gods.

'You?' Heidrun gave a sceptical snort. 'What could you do?'

'I could talk to the giants on your behalf, tell them what you have to offer. I'm heading to Jotunheim anyway. I owe Angrboda a visit. She's the giantess mother of my kids Fenris, Jormungand and Hel,' he supplied upon seeing their blank expressions.

The goat, the stag and the enormous food supply exchanged glances. 'Give us a minute,' Heidrun said.

'Take all the time you want. I'll be over here.'

Whistling, Loki strolled across the room to the thanes' table, looking for all the worlds as if he couldn't care less what they decided. Secretly, however, he very much wanted them to agree, for he planned to use the animals' enquiry as an opportunity to find out if the giants were willing to spare non-giants on the day of doom. Loki intended to be among those spared, no matter whose side he was fighting on come Ragnarok.

Meanwhile, the three creatures talked it over. None of them trusted Loki, but, as they couldn't leave Laeradr themselves, they decided they had no choice.

'We give you permission to tell the giants what we have to offer,' Ike said.

'Then I'll be on my way.' Loki vanished.

No sooner had he left than Odin himself appeared. From his all-seeing throne, Hlidskjalf, he'd heard what had transpired, and he was troubled.

'Have you learned nothing after living

aeons among einherjar?' he demanded. 'You would rather betray those who have given you a home than die a noble death defending that home?'

The beasts bowed their heads. Like a well-aimed arrow, Odin's accusation had hit its mark. They vowed then and there to stand with the gods and think no more of the giants – and so they have done.

As for Loki, his destiny was determined long before his meeting the animals. Nothing he said or did would change what fate had in store.

SLEIPNIR

CATEGORY: Notable

HOME WORLD: Asgard

APPEARANCE: Massive eight-legged horse with steel-grey hair, a white mane and black eyes

BEST KNOWN FOR: Having eight legs, being able to fly despite being wingless and belonging to Odin

MY DAD'S MOM

by Stanley, Son of Sleipnir

(translated via a horse whisperer)

Most of you think Loki is 100 per cent bad and, like, always messing things up for the gods. That is so not true. One time, she helped Odin and the others out of a huge problem.

That's right; I said *she*. Loki is my grandmother. I'll give you a moment to process that before I go on.

Ready? Okay, here's what happened:

Long ago, a builder came to Asgard. He offered to surround the world with a wall to protect the gods from attack. He said he could build the wall in three seasons, and he wanted Freya, the sun and the moon in exchange. Freya said no way. The sun and the moon took her side. Loki, though, thought the wall was a great idea. He convinced the other deities to make a counter-offer. If the builder could finish the wall in one season, he could have what he asked for. The task was impossible, Loki pointed out, so Freya, the sun and the moon would be safe. And so would the gods, because the Aesir would have at least part of a wall.

The gods proposed the plan to the builder. He agreed to the terms and went to work.

What the Aesir didn't realize was that the builder – probably a giant in disguise – had the strongest, fastest and hardest-working stallion in the worlds to help him. As the season wound down, the fortification neared completion. Freya was a wreck. The sun and the moon weren't too happy, either. Everyone blamed Loki.

Loki owned up to his mistake and set about making things right. Since the stallion was the problem, he figured out a way to get rid of it. He shape-shifted into a gorgeous mare. One flirtatious flick of the mane and coy bat of the eye later and that stallion was smitten. When Loki took off for the woods, the stallion gave chase – and that was that.

Without his helper, the builder couldn't finish the wall by the deadline. Freya, the sun and the moon stayed right where they were. And some time later Loki the mare gave birth to my dad.

So you see? Loki's not *all* bad.

JORMUNGAND

CATEGORY: Notable

HOME WORLD: Seas of Jotunheim

APPEARANCE: A poison-shooting snake. Mottled skin of yellow, brown and green. Enormous green eyes. Ridged forehead. Snub-nosed snout. Rows of sharp teeth. And a really, really long legless body.

BEST KNOWN FOR: Encircling Midgard and biting its own tail. Prophesied to consume Thor at Ragnarok.

MUSIC HATH CHARMS
by Njord

If Jormungand ever fully awakens, he'll thrash so violently that tsunamis will swamp the shorelines throughout Midgard. So, whenever the World Serpent seems restless, a group of my einherjar descendants – the only ones who can safely traverse the seas at such a time – race out to the oceans, dive deep below the surface and sing him these lullabies. My son, Frey, helped write them, so they are infused with the peace and warmth needed for a sound sleep.

As an interesting side note, humans overheard these songs at some point in history. They adapted the melodies but replaced the original lyrics with their own. Einherjar may recognize the Midgard versions.

MIDGARD VERSIONS

Slumber, slumber, Jormungand,

> (*Twinkle, twinkle, little star*)

On seaweed beds so far from land.

> (*How I wonder what you are.*)

Sleep forever peacefully

> (*Up above the world so high*)

Deep within the Midgard sea.

> (*Like a diamond in the sky.*)

Slumber, slumber, Jormungand,

> (*Twinkle, twinkle, little star*)

Nestled deep within the sand.

> (*How I wonder what you are.*)

Bite your tail, Jorry,

> (*Rock-a-bye, baby,*)

Under the waves.

> (*In the treetop.*)

No need to surface.

> (*When the wind blows*)

Avoid the sun's rays.

> (*The cradle will rock.*)

Cuddle an urchin,

        (When the bough breaks)

Snuggle a shark.

        (The cradle will fall.)

Just stay down below

        (And down will come baby)

And sleep in the dark.

        (Cradle and all.)

Please stay sleeping, please stay sleeping,

        (Are you sleeping, are you sleeping,)

Jormungand, Jormungand!

        (Brother John, Brother John?)

Shut your eyes so tightly!

        (Morning bells are ringing!)

Snooze all day and nightly!

        (Morning bells are ringing!)

Don't wake up. Don't wake up.

        (Ding ding dong. Ding ding dong.)

FENRIS WOLF

CATEGORY: Unbelievably regrettable

HOME WORLD: Island of *Lyngvi*

APPEARANCE: Grey and black fur, powerful build, fangs and blue eyes. Normal size for a typical wolf, but has an extra-intelligent glint in his eyes.

BEST KNOWN FOR: Terrifying savagery. Being restrained by the rope Gleipnir. Signalling the start of Ragnarok upon being freed from that rope.

THE INTERVIEW I DIDN'T WANT TO DO

by Snorri Sturluson

I want it on record that I never intended to go anywhere near the Island of Lyngvi, and I *certainly* had no interest in talking to the beast that's trapped there. I didn't realize that's where Hotel Valhalla's fold-out boat had dropped me until it was too late. So, if the following transcript of our conversation seems a little unprofessional at times, keep in mind that I was wholly unprepared.

SNORRI STURLUSON: Wait a minute. This isn't Norumbega.

FENRIS WOLF: Hello, Snorri.

SS [runs around in circles, screaming]: Where's the boat? Where's the boat?

FW: Nice of you to drop by.

SS [falls to knees]: Gods help me! Someone get me out of here!

FW: We never talk any more. How've you been?

SS [covers head with arms and moans]:
Leave me alone. I have nothing to say to you.

FW: That hurts me, Snorri. It really does.
Here I'm thinking, wow, a thane has come to
see me. Not even the gods do that. He must
be more courageous than they are. [Editor's
Note: At this point, the raven records that Snorri
stopped moaning and started tuning in to what
Fenris Wolf was saying.] But you're just like the
rest of them. [Hunches shoulders and hangs
head.] Aw, why do I even bother.

SS: I – I'm sorry. It's just, well, I was
tricked into coming here.

FW [gestures at Gleipnir with snout]: Just
as I was. We're a lot alike, you and I.

SS: Except I'm a human and you're a
wolf.

FW: Technicalities. We're alike where
it counts. In here. [Restraint interferes with
attempt to tap chest.] Darn this rope. It ruined
a special moment for us.

SS [shuffles closer to FW]: It looks like a
nuisance. Is it really tight?

FW: Not as bad as it used to be, but it
does get in the way. What can I do, though?

No one is brave enough to come near me and untie it.

SS [moves closer still]: I'm brave. You said so yourself.

FW [widens eyes]: You're right! Guess that makes you brave *and* smart. But I bet you hear that all the time back in Valhalla.

SS: Oh, not as much as you'd think.

FW: Go on. Good-looking thane like you? Those Valkyries probably flit about you like bees around honey.

SS [blushes]. No. Well. Maybe a few.

FW: I knew it! And I know something that would *really* impress them. You could . . . nah, you wouldn't do it. Never mind.

SS: What? What were you going to say?

FW: No, it's too much to ask. Forget it.

SS: Seriously, tell me. I insist.

FW: Well, if you insist. I was just thinking, you being such a smart, brave, good-looking thane, if anybody could figure out how to untie this old rope, it'd be you.

SS: Oh. Um, gee, I don't know if I should. I mean, the gods bound you in it for a good reason. Didn't they?

FW: Oh, sure, sure. Assuming being true to myself was a good reason, that is. Was it my fault that I was a boisterous pup who liked to wrestle and play tug-of-war, or that I grew up to be a strong, fierce fighter? You'd think those traits would be appreciated in Asgard, not punished.

SS: Is that why you're here? I could have sworn –

FW [turns his back]: Listen, just forget I asked, all right? I took you for a guy who stood for decency and fairness. I read you wrong. My mistake.

SS: But –

FW: I thought we had something in common, seeing as how you were hoodwinked into coming here by the gods just like I was. Again, my mistake.

SS: Well, maybe I could just loosen one knot.

FW: I don't even want you to do it now.

SS [stands]: That's too bad, mister, because I'm going to!

FW: Seriously, don't come near me.

SS: You can't stop me!

FW: I'm warning you, you come one step closer and I won't be held responsible for my actions!

SS: Get ready to do your worst, then, because here I come!

[Editor's Note: At this point, the raven stopped recording the conversation. The following is its report of what happened next.]

RAVEN: The thane had clearly fallen under the wolf's spell. A few more steps and he would have fallen into the wolf's jaws or, worse, succeeded in untying Gleipnir and freeing the beast. I prevented this by giving the thane a severe pecking, which broke the spell.

[The transcript picks up again here.]
SS [runs around screaming]:

AAAAAAHHHH! Stop pecking me!

[Pauses and looks around] Wait a minute . . .

AAAAAHHHH! Get me out of here!

[Runs screaming onto fold-out boat, which has miraculously reappeared.]

OTIS AND MARVIN

NAMES: Otis (aka Tanngnjóstr, aka 'Teeth Grinder')
and Marvin (aka Tanngrisnr, aka 'Snarler')

CATEGORY: Edible

HOME WORLD: Wherever Thor is

APPEARANCE: Unkempt brown fur, curved horns,
yellow eyes

BEST KNOWN FOR: Being a satisfying meal roasted,
grilled or stewed. Also pulling Thor's chariot.

GOAT-PLEASING RECIPES
by Marvin

Listen up, punks. I don't go in for therapy the way Otis does. If there's a problem, I head-butt it straight on. And, right now, I got a problem with you. I don't like how you treat us. Think I'm joking? Well, chew on this. Every night, it's the same thing: butcher, cook, chew, swallow, resurrect, repeat. That's fine. It's our fate to be slaughtered. Whatever. But what I want to know is, would it kill you to spice us up a little now and then? We're bored to death with being served the same way dinner after dinner! Look at it from our point of view, for crying out loud! A little effort is all I'm asking. Here are some ideas even dimwits like you can follow:

BUFFALO GOAT TENDERS

Slice us into strips. Dip us in milk and coat us with breadcrumbs. Fry us in oil on both sides. Dry us on a paper towel. Move us to a serving dish and smother us in Buffalo sauce. Serve us with blue-cheese dressing and celery.

GOAT POT PIE

Cube us. Combine us with peas, carrots, celery and goat broth. Boil, drain and set aside. Sauté chopped onion and garlic. Mix them with us and dump us into a piecrust. Cover us with another crust. Bake us in a dwarf kiln until golden brown. Scoop us into bowls and eat us.

GOAT CAESAR SALAD OR WRAP

Cook and dice us. Toss us with Caesar salad dressing, hand-torn romaine lettuce, shredded parmesan cheese and croutons. Serve us as a salad or roll us in a wrap for an on-the-go meal.

For additional recipes, consult Saehrimnir, will you? Sheesh.

HOTEL VALHALLA

A Final Word from the Manager

Dear Valued Guest:

Your journey through the pages of this helpful guide is coming to a close. Yet your existence in our world is just beginning. Exciting new adventures await you daily.* How will you die tomorrow? The next day? The ones after that? The possibilities are endless.**

But perhaps your destiny will take you in a different direction. Odin chose you once before, when he snatched you at death to join the ranks of his einherjar. He may choose you again, this time to venture on a noble quest beyond the safety of Hotel Valhalla. If he does, know this: only the best of the best are singled out for this honour. Those who return in triumph rise higher in the ranks. Some,

---

* Daily schedule of activities posted in the foyer.

** Hotel management cannot be held responsible for damage to property or body, or death by elevator.

like Gunilla, Davy Crockett, the Eriks and even, inexplicably, Snorri Sturluson, are awarded seats at the thanes' table. Those who fail, however, return in disgrace – or don't return at all, for death awaits beyond Valhalla's protection.

So, when you put this book aside and turn out the light, ask yourself this question: do you have the strength, bravery and wisdom to achieve a higher level of greatness? I emphasize that you should ask *yourself*. Know that if you ring the front desk and ask me this question, I will be forced to remind you that, while we provide additional towels free of charge, answers to such questions cost extra.

Thank you, and sleep peacefully so you can arise and do glorious battle in the morn.***

Helgi
MANAGER OF HOTEL VALHALLA
SINCE 749 C.E.

*** Wake-up calls available upon request. Press 0 and key in your room number and the time you wish to be woken by a blast from Heimdall's horn.

PRONUNCIATION GUIDE

Aegir	*AY-gear*
Aesir	*AY-ser*
alf seidr	*ALF SAY-der*
Alfheim	*ALF-haym*
Asgard	*AZ-gahrrd*
Balder	*BAHL-der*
Bifrost	*BEE-frrohst*
Brisingamen	*BREE-seeng-gah-men*
dagaz	*DAH-gahz*
draugr	*DRAW-ger*
Eikthrymir	*ACHE-thry-meer*
einherjar/einherji	*in-HAIRR-yar/ in-HAIRR-yee*
Fenris	*FEHN-rrihss*
Fjalar	*fee'AHL-ahr*
Folkvanger	*FOHK-vahn-ger*
Frey	*FRRAY*
Freya	*FRRAY-uh*
Frigg	*FRRIHG*
Gerd	*GAIRRD*
Ginnungagap	*GEEN-un-guh-gahp*
Gjalar	*gee-YALL-ar*

Gleipnir	*GLYP-neer*
Gungnir	*GOONG-neer*
Gunilla	*Goo-NEE-la*
Heidrun	*HY-druhn*
Heimdall	*HAME-doll*
Hel	*HEHL*
Helgi	*HEL-ghee*
Helheim	*HEHL-haym*
Hlidskjalf	*H'LIHD-skelf*
Hod	*rhymes with odd*
Honir	*HOH-neer*
Hunding	*HOON-deeng*
Idun	*EE-duhn*
Jormungand	*YOHR-mun-gand*
Jotun	*YOH-toon*
Jotunheim	*YOH-tuhn-haym*
Laeradr	*LAY-rah-dur*
Loki	*LOH-kee*
Lyngvi	*LEENG-vee*
Magni	*MAG-nee*
Midgard	*MIHD-gahrrd*
Mimir	*MEE-meer*
Mjolnir	*MEE'OHL-neer*
Modi	*MOH-dee*
Muspell	*MOO-spel*

Muspellheim	*MOOS-pehl-haym*
Nabbi	*NAB-ee*
Narvi	*NAHR-vee*
Nidavellir	*Nee-duh-vehl-EER*
Nidhogg	*NEED-hawg*
Niflheim	*NIHF-uhl-haym*
Njord	*NEE'ORD*
Norns	*NOHRRNZ*
Norumbega	*nohrr-uhm-BAY-guh*
Odin	*OH-dihn*
Ragnarok	*RAG-nuh-rrawk*
Ran	*RAN*
Ratatosk	*RAT-uh-tawsk*
Saehrimnir	*SAY-h'rrihm-neer*
Sessrumnir	*SEHSS-room-neer*
Sif	*SEEV*
Skirnir	*SKEER-neer*
Sleipnir	*SLAYP-neer*
Snorri	*SNOH-ree*
Sumarbrander	*SOO-marr-brrand-der*
Surt	*SERT*
svartalf	*SVAHR-tahlf*
Svartalfheim	*SVAHR-tahlf-haym*
Tanngnjóstr	*Tang-YOST-ir*
Tanngrisnr	*TAHN-gris-nir*

Thjalfi	*TH-yal-vee*
Thor	*THORE*
Tyr	*TEAR*
Utgard-Loki	*OOT-gahrrd-LOH-kee*
Vala	*VAL-uh*
Valhalla	*Val-HAHL-uh*
Valkyrie	*VAL-kerr-ee*
Vanaheim	*VAN-uh-haym*
Vanir	*Vah-NEER*
Yggdrasil	*IHG-druh-sihl*
Ymir	*EE-meer*

GLOSSARY

AEGIR – lord of the waves

AESIR – gods of war, close to humans

ALF SEIDR – elf magic

ALFHEIM – the home of the light elves

ANGRBODA – the giantess mother of Fenris Wolf,
 Jormungand and Hel, with Loki

ASGARD – the home of the Aesir

BALDER – god of light; the second son of Odin and
 Frigg, and brother of Hod. Frigg made all earthly
 things swear to never harm her son, but she forgot
 about mistletoe. Loki tricked Hod into killing
 Balder with a dart made of mistletoe.

BIFROST – the rainbow bridge leading from Asgard
 to Midgard

BRISINGAMEN – Freya's signature piece of jewellery,
 a ruby-and-diamond lacework necklace of
 unsurpassed beauty

BROKKR AND SINDRI – the dwarves who made Thor's
 hammer, Mjolnir

EIKTHRYMIR – a stag in the Tree of Laeradr whose
 horns spray water non-stop that feeds every river
 in every world

EINHERJAR (EINHERJI, sing.) – great heroes who have died with bravery on Earth; soldiers in Odin's eternal army; they train in Valhalla for Ragnarok, when the bravest of them will join Odin against Loki and the giants in the battle at the end of the world

FENRIS WOLF – an invulnerable wolf born of Loki's affair with a giantess; his mighty strength strikes fear even in the gods, who keep him tied to a rock on an island. He is destined to break free on the day of Ragnarok.

FJALAR AND GJALAR – two nasty dwarves who killed Kvasir

FOLKVANGER – the Vanir afterlife for slain heroes, ruled by the goddess Freya

FREY – the god of spring and summer; the sun, the rain and the harvest; abundance and fertility, growth and vitality. Frey is the twin brother of Freya and, like his sister, is associated with great beauty. He is lord of Alfheim.

FREYA – the goddess of love; twin sister of Frey; ruler of Folkvanger

FRIGG – goddess of marriage and motherhood; Odin's wife and the queen of Asgard; mother of Balder and Hod

GERI AND FREKI – two wolves who often accompany Odin

GINNUNGAGAP – the primordial void; a mist that obscures appearances

GLEIPNIR – a rope made by dwarves to keep Fenris Wolf in bondage

GUNGNIR – Odin's staff

HEIDRUN – the goat in the Tree of Laeradr whose milk is brewed for the magical mead of Valhalla

HEIMDALL – god of vigilance and the guardian of the Bifrost, the gateway to Asgard

HEL – goddess of the dishonourable dead; born of Loki's affair with the giantess Angrboda

HELHEIM – the underworld, ruled by Hel and inhabited by those who died in wickedness, old age or illness

HLIDSKJALF – the High Seat of Odin

HOD – Balder's blind brother

HONIR – an Aesir god who, along with Mimir, traded places with Vanir gods Frey and Njord at the end of the war between the Aesir and the Vanir

HUGINN AND MUNINN – two ravens who bring Odin information from all over Midgard

IDUN – a goddess who distributes the apples of immortality that keep the gods young and spry

JORMUNGAND – the World Serpent, born of Loki's affair with a giantess; his body is so long it wraps around the earth

JOTUN – giant

JOTUNHEIM – the home of the giants

KVASIR – a wise god born of the saliva of the Aesir and the Vanir

LOKI – god of mischief, magic and artifice; the son of two giants; adept with magic and shape-shifting. He is alternatively malicious and heroic to the Asgardian gods and to humankind. Because of his role in the death of Balder, Loki was chained by Odin to three giant boulders with a poisonous serpent coiled over his head. The venom of the snake occasionally irritates Loki's face, and his writhing is the cause of earthquakes.

LYNGVI – the Isle of Heather, where Fenris Wolf is bound; the island's location shifts every year as the branches of Yggdrasil sway in the winds of the void. It only surfaces during the first full moon of each year.

MAGNI AND MODI – Thor's favourite sons, fated to survive Ragnarok

MIDGARD – the home of humans

MIMIR – an Aesir god who, along with Honir, traded

places with Vanir gods Frey and Njord at the end
of the war between the Aesir and the Vanir. When
the Vanir didn't like his counsel, they cut off his
head and sent it to Odin. Odin placed the head in
a magical well, where the water brought it back to
life, and Mimir soaked up all the knowledge of the
World Tree.

MJOLNIR – Thor's hammer

MUSPELLHEIM – the home of the fire giants and
demons

NARVI – one of Loki's sons, disembowelled by his
brother Vali, who was turned into a wolf after
Loki killed Balder

NIDAVELLIR – the home of the dwarves

NIDHOGG – the dragon that lives at the bottom of the
World Tree and chews on its roots

NIFLHEIM – the world of ice, fog and mist

NJORD – god of ships, sailors and fishermen; father
of Frey and Freya

NORNS – three sisters who control the destinies of
both gods and humans

ODIN – the 'All-Father' and king of the gods; the god
of war and death, but also poetry and wisdom.
By trading one eye for a drink from the Well of
Wisdom, Odin gained unparalleled knowledge.

He has the ability to observe all the Nine Worlds from his throne in Asgard; in addition to his great hall, he also resides in Valhalla with the bravest of those slain in battle.

RAGNAROK – the Day of Doom or Judgment, when the bravest of the einherjar will join Odin against Loki and the giants in the battle at the end of the world

RAN – goddess of the sea; wife of Aegir

RATATOSK – an invulnerable squirrel that constantly runs up and down the World Tree carrying insults between the eagle that lives at the top and Nidhogg, the dragon that lives at the roots

RED GOLD – the currency of Asgard and Valhalla

SAEHRIMNIR – the magical beast of Valhalla; every day it is killed and cooked for dinner and every morning it is resurrected; it tastes like whatever the diner wants

SESSRUMNIR – the Hall of Many Seats, Freya's mansion in Folkvanger

SIF – Thor's wife

SKIRNIR – a god; Frey's servant and messenger

SLEIPNIR – Odin's eight-legged steed; only Odin can summon him; one of Loki's children

SNORRI STURLUSON – an Icelandic historian, poet
and author of *The Prose Edda*

SUMARBRANDER – the Sword of Summer

SURT – lord of Muspellheim

SVARTALF – dark elf, a subset of dwarves

TANNGNJÓSTR AND TANNGRISNR – Thor's goats, who
pull his chariot and also supply him with daily
sustenance; after being killed, cooked and eaten,
they can resurrect themselves eternally

THANE – a lord of Valhalla

THJAZI – a giant who kidnapped Idun

THOR – god of thunder, son of Odin.
Thunderstorms are the earthly effects of Thor's
mighty chariot rides across the sky, and lightning
is caused by hurling his great hammer, Mjolnir.

TREE OF LAERADR – a tree in the centre of the Feast
Hall of the Slain in Valhalla containing immortal
animals that have particular jobs

TYR – god of courage, law and trial by combat; he
lost a hand to Fenris's bite when the Wolf was
restrained by the gods

ULLER – the god of snowshoes and archery

UTGARD-LOKI – the most powerful sorcerer of
Jotunheim; king of the mountain giants

VALHALLA – paradise for warriors in the service of
  Odin
VALI – Loki's son, who was turned into a wolf after
  Loki killed Balder; as a wolf he disembowelled his
  brother Narvi before he was gutted himself
VALKYRIE – Odin's shield maidens who choose slain
  heroes to bring to Valhalla
VANAHEIM – the home of the Vanir
VANIR – gods of nature; close to elves
YGGDRASIL – the World Tree
YMIR – the largest of the giants; father to both
  the giants and the gods. He was killed by Odin
  and his brothers, who used his flesh to create
  Midgard. This act was the genesis of the cosmic
  hatred between the gods and the giants.

MAGNUS CHASE

The Gods of Asgard Arise

A breathtaking new series
featuring the gods of Norse mythology

RICK RIORDAN

EPIC HEROES · LEGENDARY ADVENTURES

COMING IN AUTUMN 2016

MAGNUS CHASE

AND THE
HAMMER OF THOR

ONE

Could You Please Stop Killing My Goat?

LESSON LEARNED: if you take a Valkyrie out for coffee, you'll get stuck with the cheque and a dead body.

I hadn't seen Samirah al-Abbas in almost six weeks, so when she called out of the blue and said we needed to talk about a matter of life and death I agreed right away.

(Technically I'm already dead, which means the whole life-and-death thing didn't apply, but still . . . Sam sounded anxious.)

She hadn't yet arrived when I got to the Thinking Cup on Newbury Street. The place was packed as usual, so I queued up for coffee. A few seconds later, Sam flew in, *literally*, right over the heads of the café patrons.

Nobody batted an eye. Regular mortals aren't good at processing magical stuff, which is fortunate, because otherwise Bostonians would spend most of their time running around in a panic from giants, trolls, ogres and *einherjar* with battleaxes and lattes.

Sam landed next to me in her school uniform – white sneakers, khaki slacks and a long-sleeve navy shirt with the KING ACADEMY logo. A green hijab covered her hair. An axe hung from her belt. I was pretty sure the axe wasn't standard dress code.

As glad as I was to see her, I noted that the skin under her eyes was darker than usual. She was swaying on her feet.

'Hey,' I said. 'You look terrible.'

'Nice to see you, too, Magnus.'

'No, I mean . . . not terrible like *different than normal* terrible. Just terrible like exhausted.'

'Should I get you a shovel so you can dig that hole a little deeper?'

I raised my hands in surrender. 'Where have you been the last month and a half?'

Her shoulders tightened. 'My workload this semester has been killing me. I'm tutoring kids after school. Then, as you might remember, there's my part-time job reaping souls of the dead and running top-secret missions for Odin.'

'You kids today and your busy schedules.'

'On top of all that . . . there's flight school.'

'Flight school?' We shuffled forward with the line. 'Like *aeroplanes*?'

I knew Sam's goal was to become a professional pilot someday, but I hadn't realized she was already taking lessons. 'You can *do* that at sixteen?'

Her eyes sparkled with excitement. 'My grandparents could never have afforded it, but the Fadhlans have this friend who runs a flight school. They finally convinced Jid and Bibi –'

'Ah.' I grinned. 'So the lessons were a gift from Amir.'

Sam blushed. She's the only teenager I know who has a *betrothed*, and it's cute how flustered she gets when she talks about Amir Fadhlan.

'Those lessons were the most thoughtful, the most considerate . . .' She sighed wistfully. 'But enough of that. I didn't bring you here to talk about my schedule. We have an informant to meet.'

'An informant?'

'This could be the break I've been waiting for. If his information is good –'

Sam's phone buzzed. She fished it out of her pocket, checked the screen and cursed. 'I have to go.'

'You just got here.'

'Valkyrie business. Possible code three-eight-one: heroic death in progress.'

'You're making that up.'

'I'm not.'

'So . . . what, somebody thinks they're about to die and they text you *"Going down! Need Valkyrie ASAP!"* followed by a bunch of sad-face emoticons?'

'I seem to recall taking *your* soul to Valhalla. You didn't text me.'

'No, but I'm special.'

'Just get a table outside,' she said. 'Meet my informant. I'll be back as soon as I can.'

'I don't even know what your informant looks like.'

'You'll recognize him when you see him,' Sam promised. 'Be brave. Also, get me a scone.'

She flew out of the shop like Super Muslima, leaving me to pay for our order.

HOW DO YOU PUNISH AN IMMORTAL?
BY MAKING HIM HUMAN.

Rick Riordan returns to Camp Half-Blood
in his incredible new series!

THE HIDDEN ORACLE

THE ADVENTURE NEVER STOPS ...

PERCY JACKSON

THE GREEK GODS ARE ALIVE AND KICKING!

They still fall in love with mortals and bear children with immortal blood in their veins. When Percy Jackson learns he's the son of Poseidon, god of the sea, he must travel to Camp Half-Blood – a secret base dedicated to the training of young demigods.

The Percy Jackson series:

PERCY JACKSON AND THE LIGHTNING THIEF
PERCY JACKSON AND THE SEA OF MONSTERS
PERCY JACKSON AND THE TITAN'S CURSE
PERCY JACKSON AND THE BATTLE OF THE LABYRINTH
PERCY JACKSON AND THE LAST OLYMPIAN

THE DEMIGOD FILES

PERCY JACKSON AND THE GREEK GODS
PERCY JACKSON AND THE GREEK HEROES

HEROES OF OLYMPUS

PERCY JACKSON IS BACK!

Percy and his old friends from Camp Half-Blood join forces with new Roman demigods from Camp Jupiter for a deadly new mission: to prevent the all-powerful Earth Mother, Gaia, from awakening from her millennia-long sleep to bring about the end of the world.

The Heroes of Olympus series:

THE LOST HERO
THE SON OF NEPTUNE
THE MARK OF ATHENA
THE HOUSE OF HADES
THE BLOOD OF OLYMPUS

THE DEMIGOD DIARIES

THE TRIALS OF APOLLO

AN OLYMPIAN HAS FALLEN!

The god Apollo has been cast down from Olympus in the body of a teenage boy. With the help of friends like Percy Jackson and familiar faces from Camp Half-Blood, he must complete a series of harrowing trials to save the world from a dangerous new enemy.

The Trials of Apollo series:

THE HIDDEN ORACLE

THE KANE CHRONICLES

THE GODS OF EGYPT AWAKEN!

When an explosion shatters the ancient Rosetta Stone and unleashes Set, the Egyptian god of chaos, only Carter and Sadie Kane can save the day. Their quest takes the pair around the globe in a battle against the gods of Ancient Egypt.

The Kane Chronicles series:

THE RED PYRAMID
THE THRONE OF FIRE
THE SERPENT'S SHADOW

MAGNUS CHASE

THE GODS OF ASGARD ARISE!

After being killed in battle with a fire giant, Magnus Chase finds himself resurrected in Valhalla as one of the chosen warriors of the Norse god Odin. The gods of Asgard are preparing for Ragnarok – the Norse doomsday – and Magnus has a leading role . . .

The Magnus Chase series:

MAGNUS CHASE AND THE SWORD OF SUMMER

Find out more at www.rickriordan.co.uk

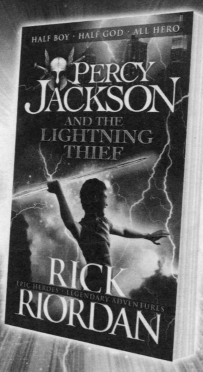

ABOUT THE AUTHOR

RICK RIORDAN, dubbed 'storyteller of the gods' by *Publishers Weekly*, is the author of four *New York Times* No.1 bestselling series with millions of copies sold throughout the world: Percy Jackson, and the Heroes of Olympus, based on Greek and Roman mythology; the Kane Chronicles, based on ancient Egyptian mythology; and Magnus Chase, based on Norse mythology. His Greek myth collections, *Percy Jackson and the Greek Gods* and *Percy Jackson and the Greek Heroes*, were *New York Times* No.1 bestsellers as well. His latest novel, *The Hidden Oracle*, is the first entry in his Trials of Apollo series, about the adventures of a Greek god cast out of Olympus and sent down to Earth as a mortal teenager. Rick lives in Boston, Massachusetts, with his wife and two sons. For more information, go to rickriordan.com, or follow him on Twitter @camphalfblood.

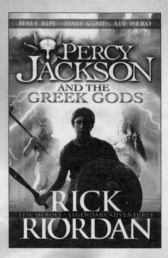
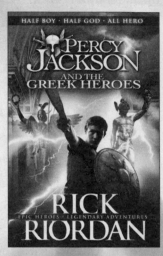